MY SiDEWALKS ON
SCOTT FORESMAN
READING STREET

Practice Book

Level
D

PEARSON

Scott Foresman

Glenview, Illinois • Boston, Massachusetts • Chandler, Arizona
Upper Saddle River, New Jersey

ISBN-13: 978-0-328-45366-5
ISBN-10: 0-328-45366-8

12 V011 17 16 15 14

Contents

	Vocabulary	Phonics	Comprehension	Writing
UNIT 1 This Land Is Your Land				
WEEK 1 Diversity	1	2	3	4
WEEK 2 Exploration	5	6	7	8
WEEK 3 Traveling America	9	10	11	12
WEEK 4 The Southwest	13	14	15	16
WEEK 5 The West	17	18	19	20
UNIT 2 Teamwork				
WEEK 1 New Ideas	21	22	23	24
WEEK 2 Working Together	25	26	27	28
WEEK 3 Team Effort	29	30	31	32
WEEK 4 A Job Well Done	33	34	35	36
WEEK 5 Our Nation's Capital	37	38	39	40
UNIT 3 Patterns in Nature				
WEEK 1 Nature's Designs	41	42	43	44
WEEK 2 Animal Journeys	45	46	47	48
WEEK 3 Our Spinning Planet	49	50	51	52
WEEK 4 Storms	53	54	55	56
WEEK 5 Going Green	57	58	59	60

	Vocabulary	Phonics	Comprehension	Writing
UNIT 4 Puzzles and Mysteries				
WEEK 1 Perception	61	62	63	64
WEEK 2 Wild Things	65	66	67	68
WEEK 3 Secret Codes	69	70	71	72
WEEK 4 Communication	73	74	75	76
WEEK 5 Finding Clues	77	78	79	80
UNIT 5 Adventures by Land, Air, and Water				
WEEK 1 Emergencies	81	82	83	84
WEEK 2 Past Times	85	86	87	88
WEEK 3 Adventures and Heroes	89	90	91	92
WEEK 4 Extreme Homes	93	94	95	96
WEEK 5 The Moon	97	98	99	100
UNIT 6 Reaching for Goals				
WEEK 1 Opportunity Knocks	101	102	103	104
WEEK 2 Challenges	105	106	107	108
WEEK 3 American Journeys	109	110	111	112
WEEK 4 Grand Gestures	113	114	115	116
WEEK 5 Space	117	118	119	120

Name_____

Vocabulary

Directions Choose the word from the box that best completes each sentence. Write the word on the line.

Tessa moved to the United States from Italy. She made new friends, but their **1.** _____ are quite different. Sometimes Tessa feels sad and **2.** _____ . The new language is hard to learn, but her new friends have **3.** _____ many words for her. Tessa wants to share her **4.** _____ with them. That way, they will get a good **5.** _____ of her home country. Tonight, Tessa is making her friends a big **6.** _____ meal. She hopes they will love Italy as much as she does!

Check the Words You Know

_ backgrounds
_ culture
_ ethnic
_ homesick
_ translated
_ understanding

Directions Choose the word from the box that best matches each definition. Write the word on the line.

_____ **7.** how you might feel if you moved to a new city

_____ **8.** changed one language to another

_____ **9.** the act of knowing something

_____ **10.** what people know and the things people have done

_____ **11.** beliefs and customs of a group of people

_____ **12.** of or about people of the same race or from the same place

Home Activity This page helps your child learn to read and write vocabulary words. Work through the items with your child. Then discuss your family's culture and ethnic background with your child. Identify special holidays and celebrations.

© Pearson Education D

Name_____

Closed Syllables with Short Vowels

Directions Write the two syllables that make up each word on the lines.

1. _____ + _____ = insert
2. _____ + _____ = ribbon
3. _____ + _____ = puppet
4. _____ + _____ = gallon
5. _____ + _____ = dollar
6. _____ + _____ = button
7. _____ + _____ = ballot
8. _____ + _____ = velvet
9. _____ + _____ = lesson
10. _____ + _____ = invent

Directions Circle the word with the short vowel sound in the first syllable. Then underline the letter that stands for that short vowel sound.

11. baseball   tunnel   lighter
12. instead   broken   super
13. music   hundred   notebook
14. collar   today   taken
15. baker   toaster   cannon

© Pearson Education D

School + Home **Home Activity** This page practices words with a short vowel sound in the first syllable, such as *happen* and *instead*. Work through the items with your child. Have your child make a collage of magazine pictures showing items that have a short vowel sound in the first syllable. Help your child label each picture.

Name_____

Sequence

- Events in a story occur in a certain order, or **sequence**. The sequence of events can be important to understanding a story.

Directions Read the passage. Then complete the diagram below.

Ming is from China. He is making a Chinese dish to share with his class. He is making dumplings. First, Ming thaws out frozen wraps. Then he cuts up chicken into tiny pieces. Next, he grates some ginger into the chicken.

Ginger is a spice used in many Chinese foods. Ming then adds herbs and other spices. He rolls up a small amount of chicken in each wrap. Finally, Ming steams the dumplings until they are cooked. They are delicious! Would you like to try some?

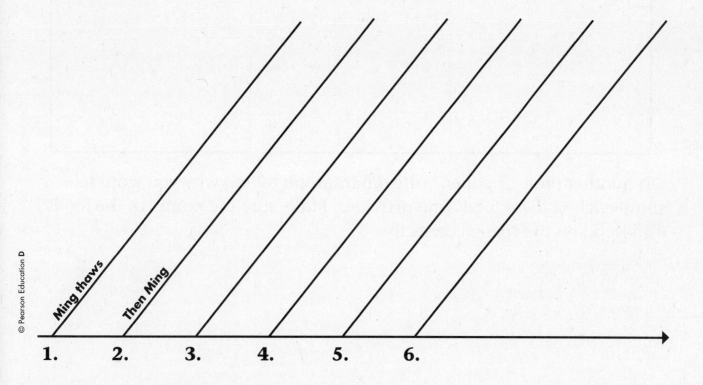

Ming thaws

Then Ming

1. 2. 3. 4. 5. 6.

© Pearson Education D

Home Activity This page practices identifying the sequence of steps in a recipe. Work through the items with your child. Then help your child make a favorite family dish. Point out how each step of the recipe is done in a certain order.

Name_____

Writing

Think about the foods you eat with your family and friends. Think about the things you do together. Which things would be fun to share with people from other countries? Write about them in the chart below.

Directions Fill in the chart with your ideas.

Food	Games	Holidays/Events

On another piece of paper, write a paragraph telling why you want to share each of these foods and activities. Make sure the names of the foods and holidays are spelled correctly.

Home Activity This page helps your child write sentences about traditions he or she would like to share with people from another country. Work through the items with your child. Then ask your child what countries he or she would like to visit and why.

Name_____

Vocabulary

Directions Choose the word from the box that best completes each sentence. Write the word on the line.

1. The map out to the country _____ us.

2. What other _____ can we use to find our way?

3. For our next _____ , we can go by plane!

4. Our country home is in a remote _____ .

5. You can get a better _____ from the top of that hill.

6. Native Americans used to live in this _____ .

Directions Circle the word that has the same or nearly the same meaning as the first word in each group.

7. **pioneers**	bankers	settlers	teachers
8. **confused**	angry	brave	puzzled
9. **area**	home	address	district
10. **voyage**	school	trip	plane
11. **device**	gadget	signal	talent
12. **perspective**	call	sound	view

Home Activity This page helps your child learn to read and write vocabulary words. Work through the items with your child. Then have your child use each word in an original sentence.

© Pearson Education D

Closed Syllables with Long Vowels

Directions Write the two syllables that make up each word on the lines.

1. _____ + _____ = reptile

2. _____ + _____ = combine

3. _____ + _____ = mistake

4. _____ + _____ = capsize

5. _____ + _____ = confine

6. _____ + _____ = dispose

7. _____ + _____ = compete

8. _____ + _____ = tadpole

Directions Add the first syllable to the second syllable. Write the new word on the line.

9. es + cape = _____

10. in + vite = _____

11. ex + hale = _____

12. ad + vise = _____

13. ex + cuse = _____

14. in + vade = _____

15. en + gage = _____

Home Activity This page practices words with a long vowel sound in the second syllable, such as *inhale* and *trombone*. Work through the items with your child. Then have your child write the words from this page. Ask him or her to read each word and then tell the long vowel sound.

© Pearson Education D

Name_____

Draw Conclusions

Directions Read the passage. Then answer the questions below.

> Josh was bored. He was visiting his grandparents, but he didn't have much to do. "Why don't you explore the attic?" his grandma asked. Josh was thrilled. Who knew what he might find? Everything looked old and dusty. Josh found a huge trunk in the corner. In the trunk Josh found lots of pictures. He couldn't believe how different people looked and dressed! He even dug up an old army uniform. Many badges and ribbons were pinned to the front. Josh felt his chest swell with pride. He knew a real hero!

1. Why do you think Josh wanted to explore the attic?

_____

_____

2. What kinds of pictures do you think Josh found?

_____

_____

3. What details support this conclusion?

_____

_____

4. Draw a conclusion about whose uniform Josh found.

_____

_____

5. What details support this conclusion?

_____

_____

Home Activity This page helps your child draw conclusions based on facts and details. Work through the items with your child. Then explore old photos, cards, clothes, or other family artifacts with your child. Talk about where each item came from.

Name_____

Writing

Think about a topic you would like to explore. Think about the things you want to find out and why.

Directions Answer the questions below.

1. What topic did you pick?

_____

2. Why did you pick this topic?

_____

_____

3. Name four things you want to learn about this topic.

    a. _____

    b. _____

    c. _____

    d. _____

4. How will you explore this topic? What will you use, or whom will you ask?

I will use _____

_____ .

I will ask _____

_____ .

On another piece of paper, write a paragraph telling why you want to explore this topic. Be sure to tell why you picked the topic and why it interests you. Reread your paragraph to check for mistakes in punctuation and capitalization.

© Pearson Education D

Home Activity This page helps your child write sentences about a topic he or she would like to explore. Work through the items with your child. Discuss with your child other topics he or she is interested in learning about.

Name_____

Vocabulary

Directions Choose the word from the box that best matches each definition. Write the word on the line.

_____ **1.** paths or plans for travel

_____ **2.** method

_____ **3.** long trip

_____ **4.** means of moving people or things

_____ **5.** units for measuring distance

_____ **6.** what you can see from a certain place

_____ **7.** a way that you choose to get somewhere

Directions Choose the word from the box that best completes each sentence. Write the word on the line.

8. Our _____ by car took seven long days.

9. How many _____ did you drive on your trip?

10. Planes are a faster method of _____ than cars.

11. Which _____ would be faster through the mountains?

12. From the peaks, you can see _____ of the valleys.

Write a Travel Diary

On another sheet of paper, write an entry from a travel diary. Imagine that you have taken a trip across the country. Write about a place you could visit. Write about what you see, smell, hear, and feel in this place.

Home Activity This page helps your child learn to read and write vocabulary words. Work through the items with your child. Then work together to come up with an itinerary for a trip your family could take. Use as many vocabulary words as you can.

© Pearson Education D

Name_____

Inflected Endings *-s*, *-es*, *-ies*

Directions Add **-s**, **-es**, or **-ies** to write the plural form of each word in ( ).
Remember that you may have to change the **y** to **i** and add **-es**.

_____ **1.** The Jones and Gomez (family) planned a trip to the Grand Canyon.

_____ **2.** We packed lots of bags and (box) into both cars.

_____ **3.** During the drive, we played games and told (story).

_____ **4.** When we arrived at the park, we set up our (tent).

_____ **5.** "What kinds of (activity) can we do here?" I asked.

_____ **6.** We can ride (donkey) down into the canyon.

_____ **7.** We can also hike many different (trail).

_____ **8.** "Tonight we can count (star)," Mrs. Gomez said.

_____ **9.** Jess and I passed out plates and (glass) for dinner.

_____ **10.** "I like (beach) better than camping," Jess mumbled.

Directions Write the plural form of each word.

11. baby _____   **13.** peach _____

12. kiss _____   **14.** truck _____

 Home Activity This page practices plurals with endings *-s*, *-es*, and *-ies*, such as *stones*, *foxes*, and *skies*. Work through the items with your child. Have your child look around your home and write a list of 20 things he or she sees. Then ask him or her to write the plural form of each word on the list.

© Pearson Education D

Name_____

Sequence

- **Sequence** is the order in which things happen.
- Dates, times, and clue words such as *first, then, next,* and *last* can help you understand the order of events.

Directions Read the passage. Then complete the diagram below to show the order of activities.

Max is planning a trip to visit his friend in New York. He is taking a train across three different states! Max has a lot of planning to do. First, he needs to make a list of all the items he wants to pack. Then he needs to gather books and music for the train trip. Next, Max needs to go shopping. He will get snacks at the store and stamps for postcards at the post office. Then Max needs to pack his bags. The last thing he needs to do is call the train station. He wants to make sure his train is leaving on time. It takes a lot of planning to take a trip!

1. _____

↓

2. _____

↓

3. _____

↓

4. _____

↓

5. _____

↓

6. _____

Home Activity This page practices identifying the order of things to be done. Work through the items with your child. Then work with your child to write a numbered list of things that need to be done on a certain day. Make sure your list is in order.

Name_____

Writing

Think about a place you have visited or would like to visit. What would you like to tell a friend about this place?

Directions Answer the questions below.

1. What place are you visiting?

_____

2. Why are you there?

_____

Directions Now write about this place using your senses.

3. I see . . .

_____

4. I hear . . .

_____

5. I smell . . .

_____

6. I feel . . .

_____

On another piece of paper, write a postcard to your friend. Describe the place using details from this page. Use capital letters for names of people and places. Make sure you have a comma after your greeting and closing.

Home Activity This page helps your child write a postcard about a place he or she has visited or would like to visit. Work through the items with your child. Discuss the proper greetings and closings for postcards using words such as *dear, hello, love,* and *your friend.*

Name_____

Vocabulary

Directions Choose the word from the box that best matches each definition. Write the word on the line.

_____ 1. taking a long walk

_____ 2. cut into another shape

_____ 3. dry, with very little rainfall

_____ 4. someone who leads or shows the way

_____ 5. farthest edge of a settled country

_____ 6. very steep, rocky slopes

_____ 7. narrow valley with high, steep sides

Check the Words You Know

__arid
__canyon
__carved
__cliffs
__frontier
__guide
__hiking

Directions Choose the word from the box that best matches the meaning of the underlined word or words. Write the word on the line shown to the left.

_____ 8. Mason was waiting for the <u>leader</u> to take him down the trail.

_____ 9. He looked over the <u>steep slopes</u> to the river below.

_____ 10. Mason knew the river had <u>cut</u> a path through the rocks.

School + Home **Home Activity** This page helps your child learn to read and write vocabulary words. Work through the items with your child. Then create an original short story together using as many of the vocabulary words as you can.

Verb Endings With and Without Spelling Changes

Directions Add **-ed** and **-ing** to each word on the left. Remember that you may have to double the last consonant or drop the final **e**.

Word	-ed	-ing
use	used	using
1. smile	_____	_____
2. skip	_____	_____
3. walk	_____	_____
4. stop	_____	_____
5. brush	_____	_____
6. cook	_____	_____
7. like	_____	_____
8. beg	_____	_____
9. clean	_____	_____
10. close	_____	_____

Directions Add **-ed** or **-ing** to the verb in ( ) to complete each sentence. Write the word on the line.

_____ **11.** Sue's family (plan) a trip to the West.

_____ **12.** They will be (drive) the whole way.

_____ **13.** Sue's little brother has (watch) many cowboy movies.

_____ **14.** He is (hope) to see a real cowboy.

Home Activity This page practices verb endings with and without spelling changes. Work through the items with your child. Then take turns thinking of action words to use in the sentence frames: *Yesterday, I ____ . Today, I am ____ .* Have your child write the word for each action, such as: *Yesterday, I <u>talked</u>. Today, I am talking.*

Name_____

Compare and Contrast

- To **compare and contrast** means to tell how two or more things are alike and different.
- Clue words such as *like* and *as* can show similarities. Clue words such as *however* and *instead* can show differences.

Directions Read the passage. Then answer the questions below.

A desert has a very dry environment. Rain is rare. But the desert is thriving with many different plants. How do they survive? Desert plants have adapted in amazing ways! Most non-desert plants use up water quickly and lose it through their leaves. Desert plants, such as cacti, have a special place for storing water. Cacti also have thorns rather than leaves, and thorns don't give off as much water as leaves. Thorns also protect the plant from animals. Most non-desert plants need water often. But desert plants can live without water for a long time. Unlike non-desert plants, they don't die. Cacti have long roots that stay close to the surface. When rain comes, the roots soak up the water and the plants spring to life! Non-desert plants find water with roots that reach deep in the earth during dry times.

1. What do desert plants and non-desert plants need to survive?

_____

2. How does a non-desert plant lose water?

_____

3. What parts does a desert plant have to help it save water?

_____

4. Describe how roots of a non-desert plant and a desert plant differ.

_____

_____

Home Activity This page practices comparing and contrasting plants from different environments. Work through the items with your child. Then ask your child to put the information from the passage into a chart. Have your child list how the plants are the same and how they are different.

© Pearson Education D

Name_____

Writing

Think about a place outdoors that is beautiful or interesting. How does it compare to the Southwest?

Directions Use the chart to compare your place to the Southwest.

	My Place: _____	Southwest
Landforms		
Plants		
Flowers		
Wildlife		

On another piece of paper, write a short essay describing your place. What makes it beautiful? What makes it interesting? Describe it using details from your chart. Then compare it to what you have learned about the Southwest.

© Pearson Education D

 Home Activity This page helps your child think of ideas for a short essay. Work through the items with your child. Then have your child read his or her essay aloud. With your child, try to think of more interesting words to "paint a picture" of this place.

Name_____

Vocabulary

Directions Choose the word from the box that best completes each sentence. Write the word on the line shown to the left.

1. Mount St. Helens is an _____ sight!

2. This volcano towers over the land like a _____ monster.

3. In 1980, Mount St. Helens shook with _____ .

4. Smoke and ash _____ a giant cloud that blocked the sun.

5. Wow! An _____ 230 square miles was buried under ashes!

6. Since that time, some trees have _____ grown back.

Directions Circle the word that has the same or nearly the same meaning as the first word in each group.

7. astonishing	confusing	smart	amazing
8. eruptions	bursts	slopes	giants
9. formed	found	forced	made
10. gigantic	scary	huge	silent
11. unbelievable	incredible	mean	interesting
12. naturally	quickly	normally	happily

Home Activity This page helps your child learn to read and write vocabulary words. Work through the items with your child. Then together discuss something astonishing in nature, such as a starfish's arm growing back or bees making honey.

© Pearson Education D

Name_____

Prefixes *un-*, *re-*, *in-*, *dis-*

Directions Add the prefix **un-**, **re-**, **in-**, or **dis-** to each base word. Write the new word on the line.

1. un- + do   = _____

2. re- + write   = _____

3. in- + complete = _____

4. dis- + allow   = _____

5. un- + cooked   = _____

Directions Write the word from the box that best fits each definition.

_____ **6.** lacking honesty

_____ **7.** fill again

_____ **8.** open a lock

_____ **9.** tell again

_____ **10.** not visible

> retell
> invisible
> unlock
> refill
> dishonest

Directions Add the prefix **un-**, **re-**, **in-**, or **dis-** to the word in ( ) to complete each sentence. Write the new word on the line.

_____ **11.** We were (able) to see the waterfalls today.

_____ **12.** The shuttles are (active) because of the storm.

_____ **13.** We will (try) seeing it tomorrow.

_____ **14.** I'll be (happy) if we miss this amazing sight.

_____ **15.** Look, the clouds are starting to (appear)!

Home Activity This page practices the prefixes *un-* (undress), *re-* (resend), *in-* (indirect), and *dis-* (disagree). Work through the items with your child. Ask your child to use each word from the box in a sentence. Then ask your child to remove the prefix from each word and use the new word in a sentence.

© Pearson Education D

Name_____

Main Idea and Details

- The **main idea** is the most important idea from a paragraph, passage, or article.
- **Details** are small pieces of information that tell more about the main idea.

Directions Read the passage. Complete the diagram by stating the main idea and three supporting details. Then answer the question.

Oregon Caves is one of Oregon's amazing national parks. These caves have been around for a very long time. The rocks that formed underground are home to many fossils. The caves have protected animals from weather, enemies, and other dangers. Ice Age fossils have been found in these caves. A jaguar skeleton was dated back 38,000 years! A grizzly bear bone was dated back 50,000 years! Over half a billion years of rock forms and movements can be seen in the cave's walls.

Main Idea

1.

Supporting Details

2.

3.

4.

5. Write a one-sentence summary of this passage.

_____

_____

Home Activity Your child used a graphic organizer to identify the main idea and supporting details of a passage. Work through the items with your child. Then challenge your child to think of other kinds of animals or fossils one might find in a cave.

© Pearson Education D

Name_____

Writing

Think about an astonishing natural place you have visited or read about. What is it like? What would you tell someone about it?

Directions Answer the questions below.

1. What is your astonishing place?

_____

2. Describe three natural things you see. Use details and interesting words. Use the words in the box to help you.

> amazing
> beautiful
> lovely
> stunning
> fantastic
> thrilling

a. _____

_____

b. _____

_____

c. _____

_____

d. _____

_____

On another piece of paper, write a postcard to a friend or family member. Describe your astonishing place using interesting words and details. Use your words to paint a picture. Make sure to use complete sentences.

© Pearson Education D

Home Activity This page helps your child write a description of an astonishing natural place. Work through the items with your child. Then together make up a fantasy story or tall tale that takes place in the area your child wrote about.

Name_____

Vocabulary

Directions Choose the word from the box that best matches each clue.
Write the word on the line.

```
Check the Words
    You Know

__awareness
__comprehend
__exhibit
__experience
__horizons
__interactive
```

_____ **1.** a special way to show things

_____ **2.** to understand

_____ **3.** what you know because you
have seen or heard about
something

_____ **4.** what is seen, done, or lived
through

_____ **5.** limits of a person's thinking, interest, and
experience

_____ **6.** having action between people or groups

Directions Choose the word from the box that completes each sentence.
Write the word on the line.

7. That _____ shows how people lived long ago.

8. Have you had the _____ of flying over the city at night?

9. Learning reading skills can help you _____ what
you read.

10. I had a greater _____ of safety rules after the fire chief
spoke to our class.

 Home Activity This page helps your child learn to read and write the words *awareness, comprehend, exhibit, experience, horizons,* and *interactive.* Work through the items with your child. Then discuss with your child what activities might expand his or her horizons.

© Pearson Education D

Name_____

Syllables with *r*-Controlled *ar, or, ore*

Directions Read the story. Underline the words with the *r*-controlled vowels *ar, or,* and *ore*. Then write the underlined word on the lines.

> This was the morning of Rosa's party. Rosa needed to buy some snacks, so she walked to the store on the corner. On her way, she saw a beautiful red cardinal in a tree. She bought popcorn, but she forgot napkins. When she came home,
>
> Rosa set up tables in the garden. She also set up a target for a beanbag toss. Rosa hoped that Jake would be her partner. When Rosa's friends arrived, Mom reminded Rosa, "Don't ignore your little sister!"

1. _____

2. _____

3. _____

4. _____

5. _____

6. _____

7. _____

8. _____

9. _____

10. _____

11. _____

12. _____

Directions Read each word and look for syllables with the *r*-controlled *ar, or,* or *ore*. Then write two more words that have the same *r*-controlled vowels. Underline the *ar, or,* or *ore* in each word you write.

13. apartment _____ _____

14. explore _____ _____

15. forty _____ _____

School + Home **Home Activity** This page practices words with *r*-controlled vowels *ar, or,* and *ore*. Work through the items with your child. Then have your child write all the *r*-controlled words from this page on index cards. Sort them into groups first by sound and then by spelling.

© Pearson Education D

Name_____

Compare and Contrast

- To **compare and contrast** means to tell how two things are alike and how they are different.

- Clue words such as *like* and *as* can show similarities. Clue words such as *however* and *instead* can show differences.

Directions Read the passage. Then answer the questions below.

Troy is a worker at the wild animal park. He went to school for a long time before getting his job. He learned a lot about lions, tigers, elephants, and other wild animals. When he leads visitors around the park, people always ask him questions. Troy most often knows the answers. But every once in a while, he has to say, "I don't know. Let me find out for you." Troy teaches people about wild animals, but he also learns something new every day.

Unlike Troy, Keisha doesn't have a job. She's only nine years old. But she wants to know more about animals too. Keisha decided to train her cat Max to do tricks. She went to the library and checked out several books about cats. She also talked to her vet. After a few weeks, Keisha got Max to jump through a hoop. Max also plays fetch and shakes hands. Now Keisha wants to train her dog too!

1. How are Troy's and Keisha's interests alike?

_____

2. How was the way Troy and Keisha learned about animals different?

_____

3. Troy and Keisha both teach. What is different about who they teach?

_____

4. Think about what Troy does for a job. Compare Keisha's interests to his. What might be a good job for Keisha when she grows up?

_____

Home Activity This page helps your child compare and contrast two people. Work through the items with your child. Then ask your child to compare himself or herself to Keisha. Have your child tell you all the ways he or she could learn something new.

© Pearson Education D

Name_____

Writing

Think about a special exhibit at a museum. What kinds of things would you see? What would you learn?

Directions Answer the following questions to describe your exhibit.

1. What is the title of your exhibit?

_____

2. List the items that will be in your exhibit. Next to each item, explain why you chose this item or what purpose it serves.

a. _____

b. _____

c. _____

d. _____

e. _____

f. _____

On another sheet of paper, describe your exhibit. Also write about what visitors to the exhibit will learn. Your exhibit should be interesting and make people want to see it.

© Pearson Education D

School + Home **Home Activity** This page helps your child write sentences about a museum exhibit. Work through the items with your child. Have your child design and draw a picture of the exhibit to go with his or her writing.

Name_____

Vocabulary

Directions Read the following passage about a baseball team. Underline the vocabulary words in the passage. Then answer the questions below.

As with all team sports, teamwork is the name of the game in baseball. A baseball team is made up of nine players. The members of the team must cooperate, or work together, to play well. A baseball team is just like an orchestra, in which each player of an instrument contributes to the music. In the same way, each baseball player must contribute to the game. What would a team do without a pitcher? What if the player on first base didn't catch the ball or tag runners? Each player has a job to do. Without collaboration between players, the team's goals could not be accomplished.

Check the Words You Know

__accomplished
__collaboration
__cooperate
__members
__orchestra
__teamwork

1. How are the meanings of the words *teamwork* and *collaboration* in this passage alike?

_____

_____

2. What does *cooperate* mean?

_____

3. Based on this passage, what is an orchestra?

_____

4. What are members?

_____

5. What does the word *accomplished* mean?

_____

Home Activity This page helps your child learn to read and write vocabulary words. Work through the items with your child. Then have your child tell you ways that members of your family cooperate and work as a team to accomplish things.

Name_____

Syllables with *r*-Controlled *er, ir, ur*

Directions Write *er, ir,* or *ur* to complete each word. Write the whole word on the line to the left.

_____ **1.** Dad took my sist_____ and me hiking in the forest.

_____ **2.** We counted th_____ty blue jays.

_____ **3.** The trail led us to a meadow full of p_____ple flowers.

_____ **4.** We ate our lunch und_____ a big, shady tree.

_____ **5.** A deer and her baby walked out and t_____ned to look at us.

_____ **6.** We did not want to dist_____b them.

_____ **7.** I used the camera that I got for my b_____thday.

_____ **8.** After lunch, we hiked down to the riv_____ .

_____ **9.** We were not in a h_____ry to go home.

Directions Say the name of each picture. Write *er, ir,* or *ur* to complete each word.

10. d_____t 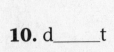   **11.** s_____prise    **12.** bak_____

13. t_____key   **14.** moth_____   **15.** c_____cus

 Home Activity This page practices words with *r*-controlled vowels *er, ir,* and *ur.* Work through the items with your child. Then have your child write other two-syllable words with *er, ir,* and *ur.* Tell him or her to underline the letters that make up the syllable in each word.

© Pearson Education D

Name_____

Draw Conclusions

- **Drawing a conclusion** is forming an opinion based on what you already know and on the facts and details in a text. Facts and details are the small pieces of information in an article or story.

- Facts and details can be "added" together to help lead to a conclusion. Conclusions formed by the author or the reader must make sense.

Directions Read the passage. Then complete the diagram and answer the question.

A wolf pack is a group of wolves that depend on each other for survival. How do wolves in a pack communicate? They howl. Each wolf has a different howl. Wolves know the howl of each member in their pack. A wolf that is out hunting alone will howl to tell the pack where food is located. A wolf that gets separated from others will howl to locate its pack. Groups of wolves will howl together as a chorus to warn enemies. This way, it's hard for other packs to guess how many wolves are in the pack. Communication is essential for keeping a pack together and safe.

Fact or Detail 1.		Fact or Detail 2.		Fact or Detail 3.		Conclusion 4.
	+		+		=	

5. What do you think would happen if wolves didn't howl?

_____

_____

Home Activity This page helps your child draw a conclusion using facts or details in a passage. Work through the items with your child. Have your child think about the way other animals communicate. Ask him or her to draw a conclusion about how this helps the animals survive.

Comprehension Draw Conclusions **27**

Name_____

Writing

Think about a special skill or talent you have. How could you use this talent to help a team or group?

Directions Write words in the chart to tell how you can use your talent. Be specific!

My special talent is _____ .

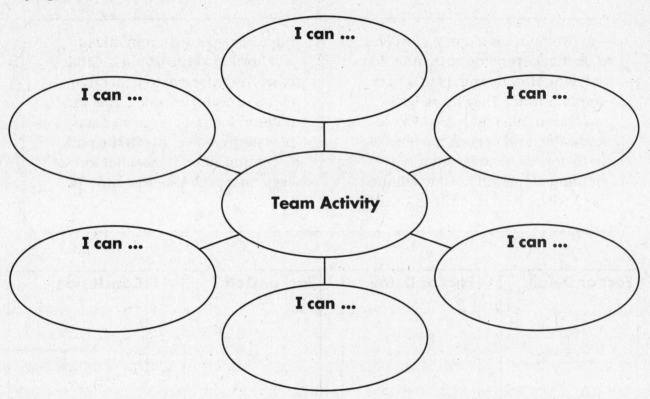

On another sheet of paper, write how your skill or talent can help the group or team. Use the ideas in your chart. Make sure to use complete sentences.

© Pearson Education D

Home Activity This page helps your child write ideas about using one of his or her skills or talents to help a group. Work through the items with your child. Then have your child explain to you how his or her talents can help a friend or family member.

Name_____

Vocabulary

Directions Choose the word from the box that best matches each definition. Write the word on the line.

_____ 1. very unusual; very remarkable

_____ 2. having or showing skill

_____ 3. wonderful or surprising

_____ 4. something that strongly affects how you feel or what you do

_____ 5. carved or modeled figures

Directions Choose the word from the box that best matches the meaning of each underlined word or words. Write the word on the line.

_____ 6. We watched the <u>very unusual</u> contest.

_____ 7. The teams created <u>shapes</u> out of sand.

_____ 8. The <u>basis</u> for one person's creation was a character from a book.

_____ 9. They used their <u>expert</u> hands to mold the sand.

_____ 10. Everyone agreed that the result was <u>wonderful</u>!

Write a News Story

On a separate sheet of paper, write a news story telling about an unusual contest. Use as many vocabulary words as you can.

Home Activity This page helps your child learn to read and write vocabulary words. Work through the items with your child. Then have your child read aloud his or her news story.

Name_____

Endings -er, -est

Directions Add **-er** or **-est** to the word in ( ) to complete each sentence. Write the new word on the line. Remember, you may have to change **y** to **i** or drop the final **e** before adding the endings.

_____ **1.** The sun is much (bright) today than yesterday.

_____ **2.** Today is a (warm) day to go outside and play.

_____ **3.** My friends and I decided to walk to the (close) park.

_____ **4.** We all decided to play the (silly) games.

_____ **5.** Everyone in my class wants to know who can tell the (funny) joke.

_____ **6.** Maybe we can see who can tell the (scary) story.

_____ **7.** We can see who can build the (strong) fort.

_____ **8.** I bet I can build a fort (fast) than you!

Directions Add **-er** or **-est** to each word. Remember, you may have to change **y** to **i** or drop the final **e** before adding the endings.

Word	-er	-est
fuzzy	fuzzier	fuzziest
9. pretty	_____	_____
10. bumpy	_____	_____
11. smart	_____	_____
12. safe	_____	_____
13. heavy	_____	_____
14. large	_____	_____

Home Activity This page practices words with the endings -er and -est, such as *luckier* and *luckiest*. Work through the items with your child. Then have your child compare different items around the house using words with the endings -er and -est, such as *That box is larger than this one.*

Name_____

Draw Conclusions

- **Drawing a conclusion** is forming an opinion based on what you already know and on the facts and details in a text. Facts and details are the small pieces of information in an article or story.

- Facts and details can be "added" together to help lead to a conclusion. Conclusions formed by the author or the reader must make sense.

S cott could not wait for the big school soccer game because he knew this year's game would be a close one. The students had been practicing since the beginning of the year. But the teachers had been practicing too. Finally, the big day was here. Out on the field, Principal Ryan blew the whistle. Maddie kicked the ball to Scott. Mrs. Copeland tried to take the ball away, but Scott quickly passed it to Jack. Jack took off down the field with Mr. Miller close behind him. Mr. Miller was fast! Then Jack saw Cameron running toward the goal, her ponytail flying behind her. "I'm open!" she yelled. "Pass it to me!" Jack kicked the ball to Cameron, and she slammed it into the net. The students had scored the first goal! *What a great team!* thought Scott, beaming with pride.

Directions Read the passage. Then complete the diagram and answer the question.

Fact or Detail 1.		Fact or Detail 2.		Fact or Detail 3.		Conclusion 4.
	+		+		=	

5. What conclusions could you draw about working together as a team?

_____

_____

Home Activity This page helps your child draw a conclusion using facts or details in a passage. Work through the items with your child. Then ask your child to share a time when he or she worked as a team. Talk about the importance of teamwork.

© Pearson Education D

Name_____

Writing

Think of an activity you did that took a team effort. Was it a success? How would you describe it to someone?

Directions Fill in the web below with all the people who worked together and what tasks they each performed. To help you describe the activity, answer some of these questions:

- What was each person's task?

- Did anyone have more than one task?

- Did the activity have a leader?

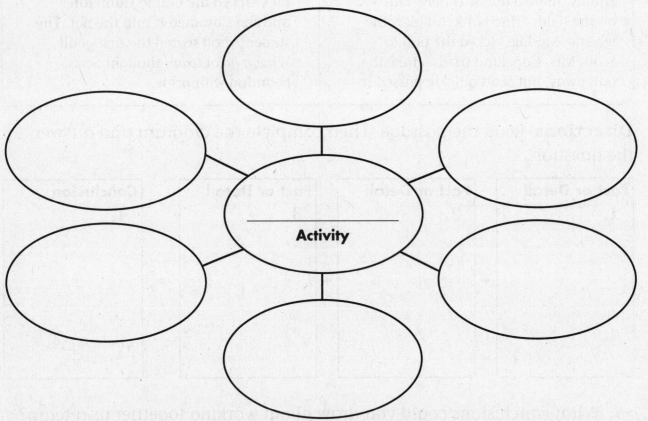

On another sheet of paper, write a description of your activity. Use words and phrases from your chart. Make sure to use interesting words and details.

Home Activity This page helps your child write a description of an activity. Work through the items with your child. Then discuss with your child how he or she feels about teamwork.

© Pearson Education D

Name _____

Vocabulary

Directions Choose the word from the box that best completes each sentence. Write the word on the line.

What kind of **1.** _____ do you want

when you grow up? If you love animals, becoming a

vet is a good **2.** _____ , or choice. Vets

make an important **3.** _____ to the

community. They help people take care of special

family members—pets! To become a vet, you must go

to school for many years, much like a doctor. And being a vet requires plenty

of **4.** _____ ! Vets must be very hard **5.** _____

because they spend long hours taking care of animals. But the rewards are

endless. Vets know they are helping animals and their owners every day.

Directions Circle the word or words with the same or nearly the same meaning as the first word in the group.

6. gear	skills	equipment	group
7. energy	strength	business	thought
8. option	an activity	a choice	a problem
9. contribution	something forced	an interest	something given
10. career	school	job	hobby

Conduct an Interview

On a separate piece of paper, write questions you would like to ask someone about his or her job.

Home Activity This page helps your child learn to read and write vocabulary words. Work through the items with your child. Then discuss with your child the types of careers he or she finds interesting and why.

© Pearson Education D

Name_____

Open and Closed Syllables: V/CV, VC/V

Directions Circle each word in the box with a **long vowel** sound in the **first syllable.** Underline each word in the box with a **short vowel** sound in the **first syllable.** Then write each word in the correct column. Draw a line between the syllables.

meter	lemon	motel	final	vanish
cabin	pilot	melon	robot	talent

Long Vowel in the First Syllable

1. _____
2. _____
3. _____
4. _____
5. _____

Short Vowel in the First Syllable

6. _____
7. _____
8. _____
9. _____
10. _____

Directions Circle each word in the box with a **long vowel** sound in the **first syllable.** Underline each word in the box with a **short vowel** sound in the **first syllable.** Then use the words to complete the sentences. Write each word on the line.

open
salad
menu
diner

_____ **11.** How long have you been working at the _____ ?

_____ **12.** At what time does it _____ in the morning?

_____ **13.** Are eggs and waffles on your _____ ?

_____ **14.** I think I will have a _____ .

Home Activity This page practices words that have a long or short vowel sound in the first syllable. Work through the items with your child. Then have your child use some of the circled or underlined words in sentences.

© Pearson Education D

Name_____

Sequence

- Events in a story occur in a certain order, or **sequence**. The sequence of events can be important to understanding a story.
- **Clue words** such as *first, after, then,* and *finally* can help you identify when events happen.

Directions Read the following passage.

Tia volunteered to help paint the school mural. It would cover one entire wall in the gym. First, the students had to vote on what to paint. Several students had come up with good ideas, but they decided that it would be an ocean scene. Outside, Tia helped mix paints in large tubs. They made different shades of blue, green, and purple. After the paints were mixed, students began drawing the mural on the wall. Then they painted over the drawing. Tia spent most of her time painting a big blue whale. The work was long and hard. Two weeks later, the mural was finally finished. The students stepped back to admire their work. A grin spread over Tia's face. It was a job well done!

Complete the time line by putting the events in the order in which they happen.

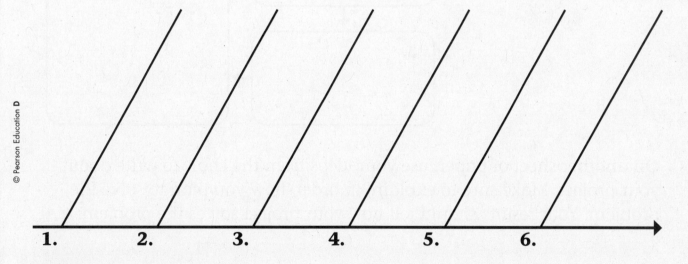

1.   2.   3.   4.   5.   6.

School + Home **Home Activity** This page practices completing a time line with the events from a short passage. Work through the items with your child. Then talk about the main events in a typical day for your child. Ask him or her to put those events in sequential order using a simple time line.

© Pearson Education D

Name_____

Writing

Think of a job or project that would help your neighborhood or community. Is there a problem that needs to be solved? It can be big or small.

Directions Fill in the chart below to tell about the project. Use words and phrases.

- First, tell about what the project is for. Tell how it will help the community.

- Then write the steps you can take to complete the project.

- Finally, tell about the results of your project. How has it helped the community?

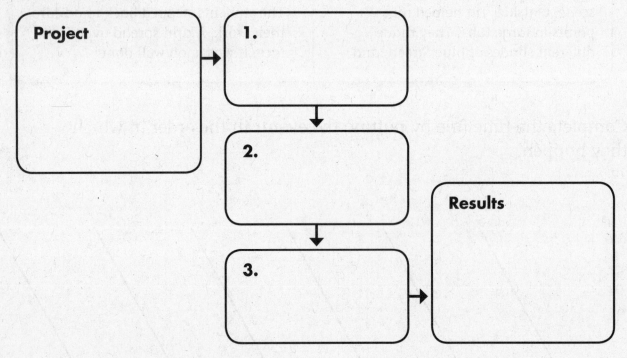

On another sheet of paper, use your ideas from the chart to write about your project. Make sure to explain, in order, how you plan to solve the problem. Your results should tell how your project solves the problem.

Home Activity This page helps your child write about solving a problem with a community or neighborhood project. Work through the items with your child. Then ask your child what household or family problems you could solve together as a team. Come up with a realistic project plan.

Name_____

Vocabulary

Directions Choose the word from the box that best matches each clue. Write the word on the line.

capital
Capitol
dedicated
executive
memorabilia
museum

_____ **1.** a building used for exhibits of valuable objects

_____ **2.** city where the government of a state or country is located

_____ **3.** set apart for a special purpose

_____ **4.** a person who manages a government or business

_____ **5.** a building where our nation's lawmakers meet

_____ **6.** things or events for remembering

Directions Choose the word from the box that best completes each sentence. Write the word on the line.

7. Washington, D.C., is the _____ of the United States.

8. We can visit a different _____ every day in Washington, D.C.!

9. Gift shops overflow with _____ , gifts, and postcards.

10. Our capital city is filled with monuments _____ to great people.

11. The _____ is the building where Congress meets and makes laws.

12. The President is the chief _____ , or manager, of the nation's government.

Home Activity This page helps your child learn to read and write vocabulary words. Work through the items with your child. Discuss the kinds of memorabilia people might gather from your own town or city.

© Pearson Education D

Name_____

Suffixes -ly, -ful, -ness, -less

Directions Add the suffix **-ly**, **-ful**, **-ness**, or **-less** to each base word. Write the new word on the line.

1. success + ful = _____

2. help + less = _____

3. friend + ly = _____

4. joy + ful = _____

5. happy + ness = _____

6. soft + ly = _____

7. age + less = _____

8. full + ness = _____

9. grace + ful = _____

10. strong + ly = _____

Directions Add the suffix **-ly**, **-ful**, **-ness**, or **-less** to the base word in ( ) to complete each sentence. Use the word box for help. Write the new word on the line.

_____ 11. The "Star-Spangled Banner" is a (beauty) song.

_____ 12. Although written in 1814, it was (final) adopted as the national anthem in 1931.

_____ 13. Be (care) not to miss seeing the flag that inspired our anthem.

_____ 14. The flag must be kept in near (dark) to preserve its color.

> careful
> darkness
> finally
> beautiful

Home Activity This page practices words with the suffixes -ly, -ful, -ness, and -less, such as *fairly, doubtful, kindness,* and *heartless.* Work through the items with your child. Then ask your child to make new words using the suffixes -ly, -ful, -ness, and -less.

© Pearson Education D

Main Idea and Details

- The **main idea** is the most important idea from a paragraph, passage, or article.
- **Details** are small pieces of information that tell more about the main idea.

Directions Read the following passage. Then complete the diagram below. Write the main idea of the passage. Then write four details that support the main idea.

The Air and Space Museum in Washington, D.C., has some remarkable exhibits. One of the most interesting is called Milestones of Flight. It depicts some of the famous "firsts" in flight and space history. The Wright brothers' 1903 plane *Flyer* is here. This is the first "real" plane to take flight. It stayed in the air for 59 seconds. Back then, that was quite a feat! You can also see *The Spirit of St. Louis*. This is the first plane to fly across the Atlantic Ocean with only one pilot aboard. *Apollo 11* is also on display. This craft carried the first men to walk on the moon! There are more than 30,000 flight and 9,000 space artifacts on exhibit. Don't miss it!

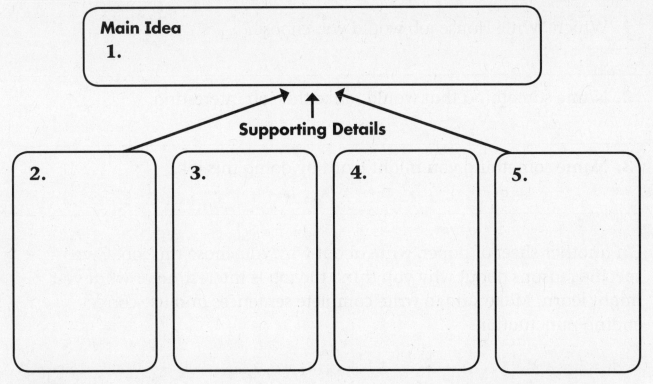

Main Idea

1.

Supporting Details

2.

3.

4.

5.

© Pearson Education D

Home Activity This page helps your child practice identifying the main idea and supporting details of a short passage. Have your child write a paragraph about his or her favorite place to visit. Then help your child identify the main idea and supporting details of his or her paragraph.

Name_____

Writing

Look at the White House jobs listed below. These are only a few of the jobs in the White House. Which job would you like to do? Why does it seem fun or interesting to you?

Chef: cooks meals for the President and important people from around the world

Chief Usher: oversees all the White House staff; makes sure everything runs smoothly

Internet Director: runs the White House Web site and oversees incoming and outgoing e-mail

Guard: also called the "secret service"; helps keep the President and his family safe

Press Secretary: directs all meetings with the news media

Directions Answer the questions below.

1. Which White House job would you choose?

_____

2. Name something that would make this job interesting.

_____

3. Name something you might learn by doing this job.

_____

On another sheet of paper, write about why you chose this job. Give specific reasons about why you think the job is interesting or what you might learn. Make sure to write complete sentences and use correct ending punctuation.

© Pearson Education D

Home Activity This page helps your child write about a White House job he or she would like to have. Work through the items with your child. Then discuss with your child some of the duties of the President of the United States.

Name_____

Vocabulary

Directions Choose the word from the box that best matches each definition. Write the word on the line.

_____	**1.** a view of scenery
_____	**2.** colors or shapes appearing over and over again in order
_____	**3.** to make something known
_____	**4.** the way something is put in a place
_____	**5.** snow that came down
_____	**6.** able to be had or gotten
_____	**7.** when something is done again

Check the Words You Know

__arrangement
__available
__landscape
__patterns
__repeats
__reveal
__snowfall

Directions Choose the word from the box that best completes each sentence. Write the word on the line.

8. A starfish and a rainbow have _____ in nature.

9. Cutting open an apple will _____ a star shape inside.

10. Tickets to the light show are _____ now.

11. The _____ of smooth hills and valleys was beautiful.

12. A shape with five sides _____ in living things.

© Pearson Education D

Home Activity This page helps your child learn to read and write vocabulary words. Work through the items with your child. Then invite your child to find an object from nature that has a pattern. Have your child describe the object's pattern using the vocabulary words.

Name_____

Long *a* Spelled *ai, ay*

Directions Write **ai** or **ay** to complete each word. Write the whole word on the line to the left.

_____ **1.** The sun is very high in the sky tod_____ .

_____ **2.** This year I will go aw_____ to summer camp!

_____ **3.** That cont_____ns all of the things I have packed.

_____ **4.** Mom expl_____ned to my brother Tim that he is too young for camp.

_____ **5.** Tim is unhappy that he has to rem_____n at home.

_____ **6.** My favorite thing to do at camp is s_____ling.

_____ **7.** We hiked in the forest and saw a fallen tree that is starting to rot and dec_____ .

_____ **8.** When school starts, I will write an ess_____ about my summer.

_____ **9.** I will also displ_____ the pictures I took at camp.

Directions Circle the word in each row with the **long *a*** sound that is **spelled the same way** as the first word.

10. tail	whale	sank	aimless
11. hail	chase	entertain	patent
12. player	snake	hurray	quake
13. mail	blade	complain	greatness
14. birthday	subway	replace	brave

© Pearson Education D

 Home Activity This page practices words with long *a* spelled *ai* and *ay* as in *obtain* and *delay*. Work through the items with your child. Then invite your child to make up silly rhymes with words that rhyme with *rain* or *play*.

Name_____

Sequence

- Events in a story occur in a certain order, or **sequence**. The sequence of events can be important to understanding a story.

Directions Read the following passage. Then complete the cycle chart below.

Grandpa told me that nature goes in cycles. He explained how the seasons affect the life cycles of plants. Because new life begins in spring each year, Grandpa and I planted a garden. I watched the seedlings grow. New buds bloomed on bushes and trees. In the summer, the hot sun warmed the Earth even more. Our plants continued to grow during the long, warm days. The cherry trees were bursting with fruit. Then, as fall approached, the days got shorter.

"That means less sunshine for plants and trees," Grandpa said. "That's why leaves change color and fall to the ground."

I loved playing in the piles of leaves! Finally, in winter, the days were very short and much colder. Our trees and bushes just seemed to stop growing. They became "dormant."

"It's like they're asleep," Grandpa said. "When spring comes, they will wake up and start the cycle all over again!"

Label each box with the correct season. Then fill in details from the passage, telling what happens in each season.

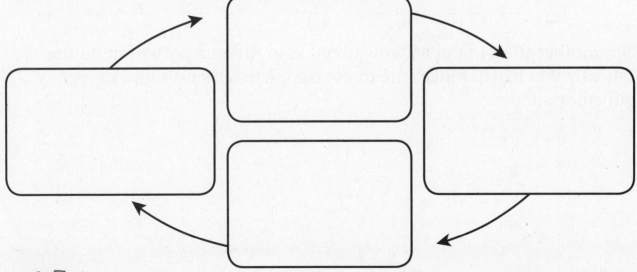

Home Activity This page helps your child identify the sequence of events in a short passage. Work through the items with your child. Then help your child make another cycle chart and write the things he or she likes to do during each season.

Name_____

Writing

Think about a pattern in nature that you have seen. It could have been a snowflake, a seashell, or a leaf. What did you notice that was special about this nature object?

Directions Answer the questions below.

1. Where were you when you saw the nature object?

_____

_____

2. What did it look like?

_____

_____

3. What kind of special designs or patterns did it have?

_____

_____

4. Name other nature objects that have a similar pattern.

_____

_____

On another sheet of paper, write about your favorite pattern in nature. Tell why you like it. Make sure to use complete sentences and correct punctuation.

© Pearson Education D

Home Activity This page helps your child write sentences about nature patterns that he or she has seen. Work through the items with your child. Then ask your child to read his or her article aloud.

Name_____

Vocabulary

Directions Choose the word from the box that best completes each sentence. Write the word on the line.

Check the Words You Know

__migrate
__observe
__refuges
__shelter
__zones

1. In the fall, some animals _____ to warmer places.

2. You might _____ flocks of birds flying south.

3. Many animals have _____ that help keep them safe.

4. Animals have living areas, or _____ , that have things they need to live.

5. Water, food, and _____ , or a place to stay, are basic needs for animals.

Directions Circle the word in each row that has the same or nearly the same meaning as the first word.

6. observe	watch	find	allow
7. refuges	talents	paths	shelters
8. zones	areas	homes	sights
9. migrate	hunt	move	feed
10. shelter	group	cover	shape

Write a Journal Entry

What do you observe in nature each day? Spend some time outdoors in a park. Write about some of the animal activities you observe. Are they finding food, shelter, or water? Write what you see. Use as many vocabulary words as you can.

Home Activity This page helps your child learn to read and write vocabulary words. Work through the items with your child. Then ask your child why family pets don't migrate. Have your child provide specific reasons.

Long *e* Spelled *e, ee, ea*

Directions Write **e, ee,** or **ea** to complete each word. Write the whole word on the line to the left.

_____ **1.** Geese fly in a V-shape and follow a l_____der.

_____ **2.** Fall is one s_____son when animals migrate.

_____ **3.** You may _____ven see them flying south in winter.

_____ **4.** When bears hibernate, they look like they are asl_____p.

_____ **5.** Then their br_____thing and heart rate slow down.

_____ **6.** Some snakes hibernate when temperatures drop below 39 degr_____s.

_____ **7.** They crawl into holes ben_____th the ground.

_____ **8.** Mayb_____ you would like them to stay in their snake holes all of the time!

_____ **9.** Are you _____ger to learn more about animals?

Directions Circle the word in each row with the **long e** sound that is **spelled the same way** as the first word.

10. peanut	sleeve	easy	leather
11. zebra	equal	weaker	better
12. eagle	head	sixteen	reason
13. proceed	scream	agree	already
14. legal	sneeze	cedar	appeal

© Pearson Education D

 Home Activity This page practices words with long e spelled e, ee, and ea as in *even*, *succeed*, and *appeal*. Work through the items with your child. Have your child read the words on the page. Then have your child change the first and last letters in *seat* and *feel* to form new words.

Name_____

Main Idea and Details

- The **main idea** is the most important idea from a paragraph, passage, or article.
- **Details** are small pieces of information that tell more about the main idea.

Directions Read the following passage. Then answer the questions.

Some birds don't migrate to find a warmer climate. They migrate to find a mate and have babies. One such bird is the emperor penguin of Antarctica. In order to migrate, emperor penguins go through amazing hardships. They will walk over 100 miles in the freezing cold and blizzards. During this walk, they do not eat and rarely sleep. After finding a mate and laying an egg, the female must find food. She walks all the way back to where she started. While she's gone, the father takes care of the egg. He must balance the egg on his feet above the icy ground. A special pouch of skin covers the egg to keep it warm. He must stand in the freezing wind and snow for about two months! The father will go without eating for about 115 days! When the mother returns with food, she takes over care of the egg. Fathers must then make the long walk back to find something to eat.

1. What is the topic of this article?

_____

2. What is the main idea of this passage?

_____

3. Write two details that support this main idea.

_____

_____

4. What would be a good title for this passage?

_____

Home Activity This page helps your child identify the main idea and supporting details in an article. Work through the items with your child. Then ask your child to compare the ways that penguin and human parents care for their children.

© Pearson Education D

Name_____

Writing

Patterns can be seen just about everywhere. Some patterns are in your classroom, such as shape patterns. Cycles are a type of pattern that repeats. Your week is a cycle of school days and weekends that repeat again and again. Patterns of events, such as day and night, can be found in the natural world. Think of other patterns and cycles that occur in nature.

Directions Use the chart to write some ideas for your list of patterns and cycles.

Animals	Plants	Weather	Other

On another sheet of paper, write a list of patterns and cycles you see in nature. You can number your list or group patterns into the different categories above.

© Pearson Education D

Home Activity This page helps your child write a list of patterns seen in nature. Work through the items with your child. Then ask your child to give you an example of each item on his or her list, such as *Animals: frog life cycle—egg, tadpole, tadpole with legs, froglet, frog, egg.*

Name_____

Vocabulary

Directions Choose the word from the box that best matches each definition. Write the word on the line.

_____ **1.** out and about at night

_____ **2.** days of rest when you are not at work or in school

_____ **3.** the act of moving along a path around a point

_____ **4.** not able to think clearly

_____ **5.** the act of spinning around like a top

_____ **6.** one half of the Earth

Directions Choose the word from the box that completes each statement. Write the word on the line.

7. My family went to the beach during summer _____ .

8. We visited a cave that had bats, which are _____ animals that hunt at night.

9. I felt _____ when I walked out of the cave into the light.

10. We went to a museum and learned how the Earth's _____ makes day and night.

11. I learned that it takes one year for Earth to make one _____ around the sun.

12. While I am enjoying summer in the Northern _____ , people in the southern half of the Earth are having winter.

Home Activity This page helps your child read and write vocabulary words. Work through the items with your child. Then ask your child to illustrate rotation by spinning around like a top and revolution by circling a table.

© Pearson Education D

Contractions

Directions Use the contraction form of the words in ( ) to complete each sentence. Write the contraction on the line.

_____ 1. (I have) been reading about the Earth.

_____ 2. Long ago, people (did not) know that the Earth spins like a top.

_____ 3. They (could not) believe that the Earth moves.

_____ 4. Today we know that the Earth (is not) still.

_____ 5. (It is) always moving.

_____ 6. We (do not) feel the Earth move because the planet is so big.

_____ 7. (We are) able to see the moon at night.

_____ 8. Because the Earth spins, (we will) always have day and night.

Directions Write the contraction form of each set of words below.

9. she will _____

10. are not _____

11. that is _____

12. were not _____

13. I will _____

14. they have _____

15. I am _____

16. you will _____

17. we have _____

18. cannot _____

19. they are _____

20. will not _____

© Pearson Education D

Home Activity This page helps your child practice writing contractions. Work through the page with your child. Ask your child to say and write three other contractions, such as *they'll, she's,* and *haven't.*

Name_____

Draw Conclusions

- **Drawing a conclusion** is forming an opinion based on what you already know and on the facts and details in a text.
- Facts and details can be "added" together to help lead to a conclusion.

Directions Read the story. Then answer the questions below.

Nicky went out at nine in the morning and saw that the sun was low in the sky. He put a paper plate on the grass. Then he poked a stick through the middle of the plate and into the dirt. The stick's shadow fell on the plate, and he drew a line along it. Nicky checked the plate every hour after that. At ten o'clock, the sun was higher in the sky.

The shadow on the plate had moved a bit and it was shorter. At noon, the sun was high above Nicky, and the shadow on the plate was very short. At one o'clock, the sun had dipped a bit, and the stick's shadow was longer. By four in the afternoon, the sun was low in the sky and the stick's shadow was very long.

1. What conclusion can you make about how the sun moves across the sky?

_____

_____

2. What facts in the story support this conclusion?

_____

_____

3. How can people use the sun to help them tell the time of day?

_____

_____

School + Home **Home Activity** This page practices drawing conclusions using details in a passage. Work through the page with your child. Then read a newspaper article together. Have your child draw a conclusion and explain what facts helped him or her to do so.

© Pearson Education D

Name_____

Writing

Think about what it would be like to have a daytime job. Now think about having a nighttime job. Write about which kind of job you would like better. Be sure to explain why you would like it.

Directions Write the answers to the questions on the lines.

What would be the pros (good things) and cons (bad things) of working during the day?

1. Pros

_____

_____

2. Cons

_____

_____

What would be the pros and cons of working at night?

3. Pros

_____

_____

4. Cons

_____

_____

5. On another sheet of paper, write about which kind of job you would like better—a day job or a night job. Explain why.

 Home Activity This page helps your child write sentences to explain a point a view. Work through the page with your child. Then discuss with your child why some people prefer working during the day while others like working at night.

© Pearson Education D

Name_____

Vocabulary

Directions Choose the word from the box that matches each definition. Write the word on the line shown to the left.

_____ **1.** away from a coast or the border

_____ **2.** something that is remarkable

_____ **3.** cannot be depended on or cannot be described ahead of time

_____ **4.** a powerful wave that forms when there is an underwater earthquake

_____ **5.** land along the sea

_____ **6.** way of acting

> **Check the Words You Know**
>
> __behavior
> __coast
> __inland
> __phenomenon
> __tsunami
> __unpredictable

Directions Choose the word from the box that best matches the meaning of the underlined words. Write the word on the line.

_____ **7.** We read about a <u>huge, powerful wave</u> that washed away many homes.

_____ **8.** The homes that stood near the <u>shore</u> were hit the hardest.

_____ **9.** Many people moved <u>far away from the sea</u>.

_____ **10.** A wave that is big and powerful is a <u>remarkable thing</u>.

Home Activity This page helps your child read and write vocabulary words. Work through the items with your child. Write each word on a card, and set the cards facedown. Have your child pick them up one at a time and give the meaning of each word.

Name_____

Long o Spelled oa, ow

Directions Choose the word in ( ) that has the **long o** sound. Write the word on the line.

_____ 1. Large crates were (stocked/loaded) onto the ship.

_____ 2. A seagull was (following/rocking) the ship.

_____ 3. All of a sudden, a wind began (moving/blowing).

_____ 4. The ship swayed (slowly/softly) back and forth.

_____ 5. A huge wave washed over the deck and (stopped/soaked) everyone.

_____ 6. The sailors started (tossing/throwing) the crates into the sea.

_____ 7. The crates (floated/bobbed) on top of the water.

Directions Write the word that best completes each sentence. Use the words in the box. Write the word on the line to the left.

| boating |
| groaned |
| snowing |
| throat |
| window |

_____ 8. My family likes to go ____ on the lake.

_____ 9. I looked out the ____ of our cabin.

_____ 10. I ____ when I saw the rain coming down hard.

_____ 11. At least it wasn't ____ !

_____ 12. Then Dad came in and said he had a sore ____ .

© Pearson Education D

Home Activity This page practices words that have the long o sound spelled with *oa* and *ow* as in *coach* and *below*. Work through the page with your child. Then give your child one minute to think of words that rhyme with *boat* and *throw*.

Name_____

Compare and Contrast

- To **compare and contrast** means to tell how two or more things are alike and different.
- Clue words such as *like* and *as* can show how things are alike. Clue words such as *however* and *instead* can show differences.

Directions Read the following passage and complete the diagram below.

People once looked at the sky to help them forecast the weather. If the sun looked dim, they thought there would be rain or wind. Certain kinds of clouds let them know it would be rainy or sunny. A red sky at night was a sign of fair weather. A red sky in the morning was a sign of stormy weather. Today, people use modern tools to forecast the weather. These tools tell how much water is in the air, the direction of the wind, and other things. People also send objects into space to take pictures of the Earth. These pictures show patterns of clouds. These patterns help people know what the weather will be like.

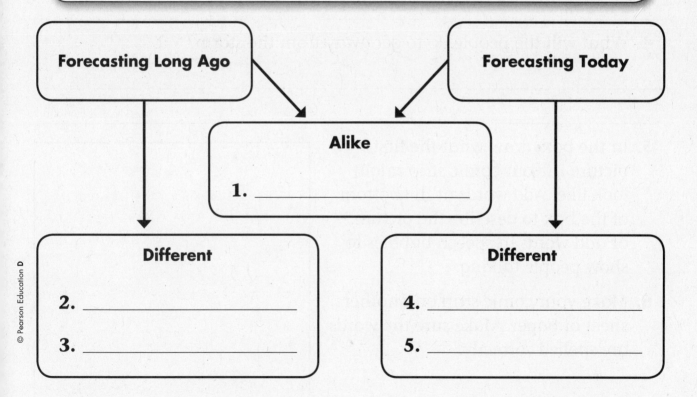

Forecasting Long Ago

Forecasting Today

Alike

1. _____

Different

2. _____

3. _____

Different

4. _____

5. _____

© Pearson Education D

Home Activity This page helps your child compare and contrast details of a nonfiction passage. Help your child fill in the graphic organizer. Have your child look at a weather report in a newspaper. Ask which kinds of information were not available long ago.

Name_____

Writing

Think about writing a comic strip. Your story will show how animals can warn people that a storm is coming and danger is near.

Directions Write the answers to the questions to help you plan your comic strip.

1. What animal(s) will you choose for your comic strip?

_____

2. Who will be the people in your comic strip?

_____

3. What will the animal(s) do to show that a storm is coming?

_____

_____

4. What will the people do to get away from the storm?

_____

_____

5. In the box, draw what the first picture in your comic strip might look like. Add words at the bottom of the box to describe the picture, or add words in speech bubbles to show people talking.

6. Make your comic strip on another sheet of paper. Make sure the words are spelled correctly.

© Pearson Education D

Home Activity This page helps your child create a comic strip about animals warning people that a storm is coming. Work through the page with your child. Then have your child read his or her completed comic strip to you.

Name_____

Vocabulary

Directions Choose the word from the box that best matches each definition. Write the word on the line.

_____ **1.** devices that can change light into energy

_____ **2.** a colorless gas that is lighter than air

_____ **3.** energy that produces light, heat, or motion

_____ **4.** things that are for the good of someone

_____ **5.** of or about the sun

_____ **6.** things that are valuable or useful

Directions Choose the word from the box that best completes each sentence. Write the word on the line. Remember to capitalize the first word in a sentence.

7. Recycling paper and cans helps to save important _____ .

8. _____ is a source of energy used to light our homes.

9. _____ of solar energy include its low cost and lack of emissions.

10. _____ is a type of gas that could be used to power cars.

11. _____ energy can be used to power and warm homes.

12. Solar _____ can change light into another form of energy.

© Pearson Education D

Home Activity This page helps your child learn to read and write vocabulary words. Work through the items with your child. Then work with your child to list ways your family can save energy around the house.

Name_____

Prefixes *mis-, non-, over-, pre-, mid-*

Directions Add the prefix **mis-, non-, over-, pre-,** or **mid-** to each base word. Write the new word on the line.

1. pre + pay = _____

2. non + living = _____

3. mis + understand = _____

4. over + due = _____

5. mid + night = _____

6. pre + heat = _____

7. over + priced = _____

8. mid + way = _____

9. non + stop = _____

10. mis + count = _____

Directions Write the word from the box that best fits each definition.

_____ **11.** to spell a word the wrong way

_____ **12.** paid before

_____ **13.** middle of the year

_____ **14.** too active

_____ **15.** not fiction

> **overactive**
> **prepaid**
> **misspell**
> **midyear**
> **nonfiction**

Home Activity This page practices words with the prefixes *mis-, non-, over-, pre-,* and *mid-,* as in *misread, nontoxic, overdo, precaution,* and *midlife.* Work through the items with your child. Then have your child list more words he or she can make with each prefix.

© Pearson Education D

Name_____

Main Idea and Details

- The **main idea** is the most important idea from a paragraph, passage, or article.
- **Details** are small pieces of information that tell more about the main idea.

Directions Read the following passage. Then answer the questions.

People use gallons of water every single day in their homes. We need clean water to drink. We need water to grow food. Plants and animals cannot survive without water. You may not know this, but fresh water is limited. But there are ways you can help conserve water. What can you do to help conserve this important resource? Here are just a few ideas:

- Turn off the water when you brush your teeth.

- Take short showers.
- Water the lawn only when it's very dry.
- Water the lawn in the morning or evening, not the afternoon.
- Wash the car only when it's really dirty.
- Keep a bottle of drinking water in the refrigerator so you will not have to run the water to cool it for drinking.

1. What is the main idea of this article?

_____

2. Write three details that support this main idea.

_____

_____

_____

3. What would be a good title for this article?

_____

© Pearson Education D

Home Activity This page helps your child identify the main idea and supporting details in an article. Work through the items with your child. Then work together to think of ways your family can conserve water.

Name_____

Writing

Think of an invention that can produce a new form of energy without causing pollution. Your invention could use the sun, wind, or water to make it work.

Directions Answer the questions below.

1. My new invention is called a _____ .

2. What materials are used to make your invention?

_____

_____

3. How does your invention produce new energy? How does it work?

_____

_____

_____

4. Draw a picture of your invention below. Label the parts.

On another sheet of paper, write about your invention. Tell how it produces energy by using the sun, wind, or water. Make sure to use complete sentences and correct punctuation.

Home Activity This page helps your child write sentences about a new invention that produces energy. Work through the items with your child. Then help your child think of ways your family can conserve energy.

© Pearson Education D

Name_____

Vocabulary

Directions Choose the word from the box that matches each clue.
Write the word on the line.

_____ 1. disappear

_____ 2. person who does magic tricks

_____ 3. full of mystery

_____ 4. not able to be seen

_____ 5. It looks different from what it
really is.

_____ 6. how we see or understand a thing

**Check the Words
You Know**

__illusion
__invisible
__magician
__mysterious
__perception
__vanish

Directions Write a word that answers each question.

7. *Invisible* has the prefix *in.*

What word has the prefix *in* and the word *correct*? _____

8. For "magic" tricks, see a *magician* (*magic* + *-ian*).

What is the word for someone who plays *music*? _____

9. A place of *mystery* can be called *mysterious.*

What can you call a place of *danger?* _____

Write a Description

On a separate paper, write what you learned by reading about the places
called mystery spots. Use as many of the vocabulary words as you can.

Home Activity This page helps your child read and write vocabulary words. Work through the items with
your child. Then help your child think of other words that begin with *in-* (such as *incomplete*) or that end with
-ian (electrician).

© Pearson Education D

Compound Words

Directions Put the two words in each pair together. Write the compound word that is made of the two words.

1. every + one = _____

2. table + top = _____

3. gentle + men = _____

4. hand + cuffs = _____

5. French + man = _____

6. ear + phones = _____

7. any + body = _____

8. air + port = _____

9. view + point = _____

10. skate + board = _____

Directions Write the compound word from the box that matches the underlined words in each sentence.

| handcuffs |
| Frenchman |
| tabletop |
| gentlemen |
| everyone |

_____ 11. Ladies and <u>men of good manners</u>, welcome to the show!

_____ 12. The prisoner wore <u>cuffs of steel</u> around his wrists.

_____ 13. Two large books rested on the <u>surface of a table</u>.

_____ 14. <u>Every person</u> in the room watched the trick carefully.

_____ 15. The magician was a <u>man from France</u> named Marc.

© Pearson Education D

Home Activity This page practices compound words. Work through the page with your child. Ask your child to say the two words in each of these compound words: *everyone*, *tabletop*, and *Frenchman*—and to say other compound words.

Name_____

Sequence

- **Sequence** is the order in which things happen in a story.
- Sometimes clue words can help you. They can tell you what happens first, next, and last. Some stories tell about the times or dates when things happen.

Directions Read this passage. Then complete the chart.

Last night, my sister Mari asked if I would like to see a trick. She said she could fill a water cup higher than the top of the cup. First, Mari filled a plastic cup with water almost to the top. Then she carried it to the freezer. She set the cup in an empty place. I made sure it would not tip over. Next, she closed the freezer and said we must wait until morning. This morning, we got up and took the cup out. The ice went above the top of the cup. I had to admit it was a good trick.

The first thing Mari did with the cup

1.

↓

The second thing Mari did with the cup

2.

↓

The third thing Mari did with the cup

3.

↓

The fourth thing Mari did at the freezer last night

4.

5. What happens in the morning?

_____

Home Activity This page allows your child to identify the sequence of events in a short story. Work through the items with your child. Then ask what steps a person could take to freeze a cup of water in a very cold city during winter.

© Pearson Education D

Name_____

Writing

Think about writing an ad. Your ad should make people want to see Houdini perform. First think of words to make Houdini's tricks sound great.

Directions Circle any words from the box that you might use. Write other words that you can use in your ad.

amazing	escape
thrill	illusion
magic	magician

1. _____ _____

Then write ideas to put into your ad.

2. Where and when will Houdini perform?

_____

_____

3. Why would people want to see the show? Write 1 reason.

_____

_____

4. Write another reason.

_____

_____

5. Write a good sentence or phrase to begin the ad.

_____

_____

On another paper, write your ad. The ad should make your friends want to see Houdini perform. Make sure names and words are spelled correctly.

Home Activity This page helps your child write sentences about a topic. Work through the page with your child. Then have your child read the ad aloud.

© Pearson Education D

Name_____

Vocabulary

Directions Choose the word from the box that best matches each definition. Write the word on the line.

_____ 1. the act or process of giving or exchanging information or news

_____ 2. an answer by saying, writing, or doing something

_____ 3. youth; offspring

_____ 4. conditions of belonging to the same family; conditions that exist between people or groups that deal with each other

_____ 5. to keep someone or something safe from harm or danger; defend; guard

_____ 6. an animal's ability to know how to do something without learning how to do it

Directions Choose the word from the box that best completes each sentence. Write the word on the line shown to the left.

7. Cats often _____ their kittens by hiding them.

8. A skunk may spray as a _____ to fear.

9. Wild animals have learned to _____ danger.

10. Howling is a form of _____ between wolves.

11. Most birds raise their _____ in nests.

12. Parents share special _____ with their children.

Home Activity This page helps your child learn to read and write vocabulary words. Work through the items with your child. Have your child think about a pet or other animal he or she knows. Write a description of the animal together. Use as many vocabulary words as you can.

© Pearson Education D

Name_____

Long *i* Spelled *igh, ie,* Final *y*

Directions Add **-ies** and **-ied** to each word on the left. Remember to drop the **y** first.

Word	-ies	-ied
terrify	terrifies	terrified
1. try	_____	_____
2. satisfy	_____	_____
3. fry	_____	_____
4. deny	_____	_____
5. dry	_____	_____
6. reply	_____	_____

Directions Circle the word in each row that has the long *i* sound.

7.	might	milk	meat
8.	where	what	why
9.	by	beach	bend
10.	hill	high	head
11.	list	lie	lamp
12.	shell	shear	shy
13.	skylight	skit	scrape
14.	trip	tied	tank
15.	seek	sight	slip

Home Activity This page practices words with long *i* spelled as *igh, ie,* and final *y*. Work through the items with your child. Then have your child write the words with the long *i* sound on index cards, and sort them into groups by their spelling.

Name_____

Compare and Contrast

- To **compare and contrast** means to tell how two or more things are alike and different.

- Clue words such as *like* and *as* can show similarities. Clue words such as *however* and *instead* can show differences.

Directions Read the passage. Then answer the questions below.

Whales are animals that live in the ocean like fish. But whales are not fish. They are mammals. They have lungs and need to come to the surface of the water for air. Whales give birth to live young. Baby whales are called calves. Mothers usually have one calf at a time. A calf stays with its mother for up to a year. During this time, the mother gives milk to the calf and teaches it how to survive on its own.

Sharks are fish, and they breathe through gills. However, unlike other fish, most sharks can give birth to live young. They can also lay eggs that hatch later. Baby sharks are called pups. Sharks can have several pups at a time. If they lay eggs, they can lay up to 100 eggs. Pups are born with a full set of teeth. They swim away as soon as they are born. If they don't, even their own mothers may eat them!

1. How are mammals and fish different?

_____

2. How are whales and sharks similar in the way they give birth?

_____

3. How are they different?

_____

4. Describe the differences between the way whales and sharks care for their babies.

_____

_____

School + Home **Home Activity** This page helps your child compare and contrast whales and sharks. Ask your child to tell you how human mothers and babies are similar to and different from whale mothers and their babies.

© Pearson Education D

Writing

Think about writing a story. In this story, a character will solve a problem and learn a lesson.

Directions Use the chart to build your story. First, come up with at least two characters. Then write about a problem that needs to be solved, the solution, and the lesson learned.

Title _____

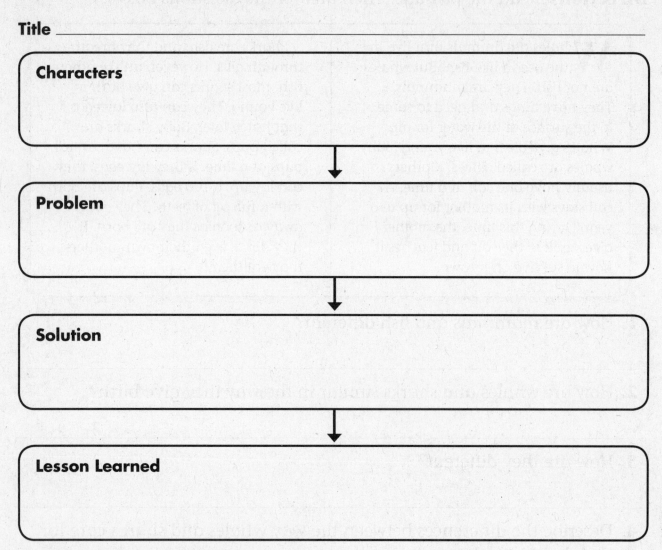

Characters

Problem

Solution

Lesson Learned

On another sheet of paper, write your story. The story should tell how a character learned a lesson by solving the problem. Make sure to use correct capitalization and punctuation.

Home Activity This page helps your child write ideas to build a story. Work through the items with your child. Then have your child share his or her story with the family.

Name_____

Vocabulary

Directions Choose the word from the box that best completes each sentence. Write the word on the line shown to the left.

_____ 1. The players use secret hand signals to _____ information to each other.

_____ 2. My dad _____ each signal and explains what it means.

_____ 3. Let's _____ phone numbers so we can call each other later.

_____ 4. She always _____ her treasure box behind the books.

_____ 5. The winning poster is _____ for everyone to see.

_____ 6. His idea for a new robot was the most _____ .

Check the Words You Know
__conceals
__creative
__exchange
__interprets
__transmit
__visible

Directions Circle the word that has the same or nearly the same meaning as the first word in each group.

7. **conceals**	finds	hides	shows
8. **transmit**	send	add	ask
9. **exchange**	call	switch	hold
10. **interpret**	explain	ask	display

Home Activity This page helps your child learn to read and write vocabulary words. Work through the items with your child. Talk about codes your child may have seen in books or on TV. Use vocabulary words to discuss how codes are used.

© Pearson Education D

Name_____

Consonant + *le* Syllables

Directions Write the two syllables that make up each word on the lines.

1. _____ + _____ = angle

2. _____ + _____ = single

3. _____ + _____ = middle

4. _____ + _____ = uncle

5. _____ + _____ = able

6. _____ + _____ = wiggle

7. _____ + _____ = cable

8. _____ + _____ = juggle

9. _____ + _____ = fable

10. _____ + _____ = bundle

Directions Choose the word in the box that matches each picture. Write the word on the line. Then draw a line to divide it into syllables.

bubble
eagle
cradle
turtle
candle

11.  _____

12.  _____

13.  _____

14. 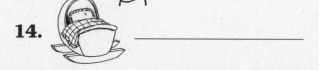 _____

15.  _____

 Home Activity This page practices words with two syllables that end with *le*, such as *bundle* and *bugle*. Work through the items with your child. Then have your child use the words on this page, or other words ending in *le* to write a silly poem.

© Pearson Education D

Name_____

Compare and Contrast

- To **compare and contrast** means to tell how two or more things are alike and different.
- Clue words such as *like* and *as* can show similarities. Clue words such as *however* and *instead* can show differences.

Directions Read the following passage. Then complete the chart by comparing and contrasting Morse code and text messaging.

Morse code is used to send messages by sound. The first Morse code message was sent in 1835. It uses long and short bits of sound to transmit letters and numbers. Morse code is a fast way to send messages, and it can be used anywhere. You do not need a radio or cell phone to send messages in Morse code. You can send messages with loud taps. But Morse code is not a secret code. Many people understand it.

Text messaging is also a way to send messages. Unlike Morse code, text messaging is fairly new. The first text message was sent in 1992. Instead of sound, people use both letters and numbers to create words and phrases. Some examples are GR8 for *great* and CUL8R for *See you later.* Like Morse code, text messaging is a fast way to send messages. However, you cannot use it everywhere. You must have a cell phone or a computer to send text messages. As in Morse code, text messaging is not a secret code. Many people understand it.

Alike	Different
1.	4.
2.	5.
3.	6.

Home Activity This page helps your child compare and contrast Morse code and text messaging. Work through the items with your child. Then work with him or her to think of other ways to send messages.

Name_____

Writing

Imagine that you need a secret code between you and one of your friends. What type of code would you use?

Directions Choose a code from the box or think of a new code. Describe your code below.

> backward
> mask
> mirror
> picture
> route cipher
> ruler
> scrambled

1. My code will be a _____ code.

2. I will make my code by _____
_____ .

Now answer these questions.

3. Who will also know your code?

_____

_____

4. How will the code work?

_____

_____

5. Use a code to write a secret message to a friend.

_____

_____

© Pearson Education D

Home Activity This page helps your child write sentences about secret codes. Work through the items with your child. Then discuss with your child how he or she came up with the code.

Name_____

Vocabulary

Directions Choose the word from the box that best matches each definition. Write the word on the line.

_____ 1. calls or yells

_____ 2. an area or a space

_____ 3. a talk between two or more people

_____ 4. to put together

_____ 5. objects or marks that stand for something

Directions Choose the word from the box that completes each statement. Write the word on the line.

6. Today I learned a new _____ that means hello.

7. People on the West Coast speak a different _____ than people on the East Coast.

8. Sometimes you can _____ two or more words to make one long word.

9. I had a short _____ with my friend.

10. Long ago people carved _____ in clay to keep records.

Write a Paragraph

On a separate sheet of paper, write a paragraph explaining how the English language grows and changes. Use as many vocabulary words as you can.

Home Activity This page helps your child read and write vocabulary words. Work through the items with your child. Then help your child list different ways he or she communicates with others, such as writing a letter or talking on the phone.

© Pearson Education D

Diphthongs *ou, ow/ou/*

Directions Circle the words in the box that have the same vowel sound heard in **out** and **owl**. Then write the words in the correct column to show if the sound is spelled *ou* or *ow*.

out

1. _____

2. _____

3. _____

4. _____

5. _____

owl

6. _____

7. _____

8. _____

9. _____

10. _____

allow	pillow
around	powder
bounce	rainbow
bowling	shower
cloudy	trout
crows	window
flower	without
growled	youth

Directions Circle the word that has the same vowel sound as the first word. Then write a sentence on the line that uses the circled word.

11. howl   throat   crown   below

_____

12. shout   your   shook   amount

_____

13. frown   tower   snowing   woe

_____

14. counted spoil   you   loud

_____

15. plow   crowd   owner   enjoy

_____

Home Activity This page practices words with *ou* and *ow* with the vowel sound heard in *out* and *owl*. Work through the page with your child. Then ask your child to write one sentence using as many of the circled words in the box as possible.

© Pearson Education D

Name_____

Main Idea and Details

- The **main idea** is the most important idea in a paragraph, passage, or article.
- **Details** are small pieces of information that tell more about the main idea.

Directions Read the following passage. Then complete the diagram below.

Long ago certain tribes in Africa used drums to "talk" to one another. These drums were called "talking drums." They were used almost like phones are used today. A skilled drummer would hit a drum in just the right way to make sounds.

The tone and the beat of the drum sounded like speech. These sounds could be heard for many miles. With a talking drum, a person could quickly "call" those who lived far away. Hearing a talking drum was like hearing someone speak!

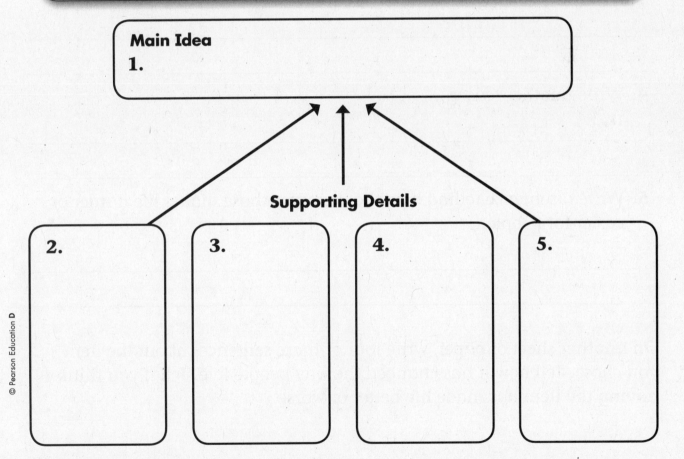

Main Idea

1.

Supporting Details

2.

3.

4.

5.

© Pearson Education D

Home Activity This page helps your child identify the main idea and supporting details of a passage. Work with your child to fill in the chart. Then have your child think of an appropriate title for this passage, such as *Talking Drums.*

Name_____

Writing

Think about what your life would be like without computers, televisions, or telephones. Would your life be harder or easier?

1. Choose one of the items in the box. Write it on the line.

| computer |
| telephone |
| television |

_____

2. Write one way your life would be different if you did not have the item you chose.

_____

_____

3. Would your life be harder or easier without this item? Give one reason.

_____

_____

4. Write another reason.

_____

_____

5. Write a sentence telling how the item you chose makes life harder or easier for people.

_____

_____

On another sheet of paper, write four or more sentences about the item you chose. Tell how it has changed the way people live. Tell if you think having the item has made life better or worse.

Home Activity This page helps your child write an opinion about a topic. Work through the page with your child. Then have your child read his or her completed pages aloud.

© Pearson Education D

Name_____

Vocabulary

Directions Choose the word from the box that best matches each
definition. Write the word on the line.

_____ **1.** to look closely in order to
find facts

_____ **2.** proof that something is true

_____ **3.** a careful study

_____ **4.** having a strong wish to
know something

_____ **5.** someone who goes to unknown places to find
new things

_____ **6.** to cause someone to believe

Directions Choose the word from the box that best matches the
meaning of the underlined words. Write the word on the line.

_____ **7.** We need to look at the <u>facts</u> before we can decide
what to believe.

_____ **8.** A <u>person who works under water</u> must carry a
tank of air.

_____ **9.** Yoko was <u>eager to find out</u> about the footprints
she saw.

_____ **10.** They will <u>carefully look into</u> the crime and
find clues.

© Pearson Education D

 Home Activity This page helps your child read and write vocabulary words. Work through the items with
your child. Then have your child use each word in an original sentence.

Practice Book Unit 4

Vocabulary 77

Name_____

Suffixes -er, -or, -ish, -ous

Directions Add the suffix to each base word. Write the new word on the line.

1. paint + *er* = _____

2. visit + *or* = _____

3. joy + *ous* = _____

4. green + *ish* = _____

Directions Choose the word from the box that best fits the definition. Write the word on the line.

_____ **5.** like a small child

_____ **6.** one who has a job helping students learn

_____ **7.** not safe

_____ **8.** a person who has a part in a play

> **actor**
> **babyish**
> **dangerous**
> **teacher**

Directions Add the suffix **-er**, **-or**, **-ish**, or **-ous** to the base word in ( ) to complete each sentence. Use the words in the box to help you. Write the word on the line.

_____ **9.** Bigfoot is a (fame) monster.

_____ **10.** A (report) wrote about Bigfoot in 1884.

_____ **11.** A train (conduct) said he saw Bigfoot.

_____ **12.** Some people think it is (fool) to hunt for Bigfoot.

> **conductor**
> **famous**
> **foolish**
> **reporter**

© Pearson Education D

Home Activity This page practices forming words with the suffixes *-er*, *-or*, *-ish*, and *-ous*. Work through the page with your child. Then let your child see how many jobs he or she can think of in one minute that end in *-er* or *-or*.

Name_____

Draw Conclusions

- **Drawing a conclusion** is forming an opinion based on what you already know or on the facts and details in a text.

- Check an author's conclusions or your own conclusions by asking: Is this the only logical choice? Are the facts accurate?

Directions Read the following passage. Then answer the questions below.

> Twins may look the same. But they don't have the same fingerprints. No two people in the whole world have the same fingerprints! Each person's prints have different traits. These traits are called ridges, spirals, loops, splits, and dots. Even as you grow, your fingerprints stay the same. Only a severe injury might change them.
>
> The odds of two people having the same fingerprints are 64 billion to one! We leave our prints everywhere. Even if we can't see them, our prints are on doorknobs, cups, and phones. Fingerprints are important clues for the police when solving crimes. Their computers hold more than 40 million fingerprint records.

1. Suppose you got a deep cut in the end of your finger. What do you think might happen to your fingerprint?

_____

2. What details support this conclusion?

_____

3. Draw a conclusion about why fingerprints are an important tool for the police.

_____

4. What details support this conclusion?

_____

Home Activity This page helps your child draw conclusions using facts and details. Work through the items with your child. Then use washable ink to stamp your fingerprints and those of your child on paper. (You can also press your fingertips onto clear tape.) Examine the similarities and differences between your sets of prints.

© Pearson Education D

Name_____

Writing

Think about a legend involving a mysterious creature or place. What makes it mysterious? What clues can you leave for the reader? Be creative!

Directions Fill in this story chart to help you write your legend.

Title

Setting

Characters

Events

First...
Clues:

↓

Second...
Clues:

↓

Then...
Clues:

↓

Next...
Clues:

↓

Finally...

© Pearson Education D

 School + Home

Home Activity This page helps your child write a legend about a mysterious creature or place. Work through the items with your child. Then invite your child to illustrate each event in the legend, creating a storyboard to share with the family.

Name_____

Vocabulary

Directions Choose the words from the box that best complete the sentences. Write the words on the lines.

A group of firefighters visited our class this

week and talked about their jobs. They told us

that fighting fires is an important

1. _____ . It can also be very

2. _____ work. Many firefighters

have gotten hurt. Once, a building that was

3. _____ almost fell on them. That was a close

call! The firefighters said that a crumbling wall is just one of the

many **4.** _____ they face. They said the most

5. _____ part of their job is when they rescue people.

I can only imagine what a thrill that must be! I think every firefighter

is a **6.** _____ .

Check the Words You Know

___dangerous
___destroyed
___exciting
___hazards
___hero
___profession

Directions Circle the word or words with the same or nearly the same meaning as the first word in the group.

7. destroyed	created	ruined	put out
8. hazards	dangers	tools	equipment
9. hero	a leader	a brave person	a happy person
10. exciting	boring	interesting	thrilling
11. profession	job	task	need
12. dangerous	small	not easy	not safe

Home Activity This page helps your child learn to read and write vocabulary words. Work through the items with your child. Then read a book together about firefighters or other heroes. Discuss the heroes, using the vocabulary words.

© Pearson Education D

Diphthongs *oi, oy*

Directions Write **oi** or **oy** to complete each word. Write the whole word on the line to the left.

_____ **1.** Josh hurt his elbow j_____nt during a basketball game.

_____ **2.** The n_____se in the gym stopped.

_____ **3.** A paramedic helped the injured b_____.

_____ **4.** The paramedic was empl_____ed by the school.

_____ **5.** He applied a cold, m_____st gel to Josh's elbow.

_____ **6.** Then he c_____led a bandage around it.

_____ **7.** He told Josh to av_____d moving his arm.

_____ **8.** Everyone j_____ned together and clapped for Josh.

_____ **9.** Josh enj_____ed the rest of the game from the bench.

Directions Circle the word in each group that has the same vowel sound as in **foil**.

10. bandage   royal   shore

11. poison   rescue   story

12. officer   visit   annoy

13. destroy   formed   supplies

14. dispatcher material   spoiled

Home Activity This page practices words with the vowel sound heard in *coil* and *toy*. Work through the items with your child. Then have your child make a list of words that rhyme with *joy, coin,* and *boil*.

Name_____

Compare and Contrast

- To **compare and contrast** means to tell how two or more things are alike and different.
- Clue words such as *like* and *as* can show how things are alike. Clue words such as *however* and *instead* can show differences.

Directions Read the following passage. Then answer the questions.

Both firefighters and lifeguards are different types of rescue workers. Although they are different, they have much in common. Both must always be ready for emergencies. Both must also have special training to help people. However, firefighters are trained to help people escape from fires. Lifeguards are trained to carry drowning people from water. Firefighters must wait at firehouses until they are needed. Lifeguards wait right where an emergency might happen. This can be at beaches, lakes, or swimming pools. Lifeguards use special equipment to rescue people, such as rescue tubes and rescue cans. Unlike firefighters' equipment, these things are light and easy to carry. They must be able to float in water. Firefighters have much more equipment, such as air packs, tools, and masks. They must also wear special clothing, such as heavy coats and pants. Lifeguards only need to wear a bathing suit!

1. Name three ways that firefighters and lifeguards are alike.

_____

_____

2. Name three ways that firefighters and lifeguards are different.

_____

_____

_____

© Pearson Education D

Home Activity This page helps your child compare and contrast firefighters and lifeguards. Work through the items with your child. Then together discuss other types of rescue workers, such as police officers and paramedics. Discuss how they are alike and different.

Name_____

Writing

Think of different possible emergencies. What can you do to be ready for them?

Directions Fill in the chart with ways you can prepare for each kind of emergency.

How I Would Prepare for an Emergency

Fire	
Choking	
Injury	
Household Hazards	

On another sheet of paper, write a fire escape plan to share with your family. Tell how to leave your home safely and where to meet your family members when you are out of danger.

Home Activity This page helps your child write about plans for emergencies. Work through the ways to prepare for each emergency with your child. Then ask your child to read his or her plan aloud.

Name_____

Vocabulary

Directions Draw a line to connect each word on the left with its definition on the right.

1. civilization

2. traditions

3. theater

4. statue

5. society

6. ancient

a place to see shows and other performances

people living together as a group

from times long past

a way of life that usually includes towns, written language, and special kinds of work

model made of metal, stone, or wood that looks like an animal or a person

ideas or beliefs handed down from one group to another

Check the Words You Know

__ancient
__civilization
__society
__statue
__theater
__traditions

Directions In each statement below, the first pair of words has a certain relationship. To complete the statement, add a word that gives the second pair of words the same relationship as the first pair. For example, *Neat* is to *messy* (opposite meanings) as *happy* is to *sad* (opposite meanings). Choose a word from the box and write it on the line.

7. *Artist* is to *painting* as *sculptor* is to _____ .

8. *Quiet* is to *noisy* as *new* is to _____ .

9. *Music* is to *concert hall* as *play* is to _____ .

10. *Cash* is to *money* as *customs* are to _____ .

11. *Invent* is to *invention* as *civilize* is to _____ .

12. *Deer* is to *herd* as *person* is to _____ .

Home Activity This page helps your child learn to read and write vocabulary words. Work through the items with your child. Together, create additional analogies, as shown in the second activity, to use with the vocabulary words.

Common Syllables
-ion, -tion, -sion, -ture

Directions Add **-ion**, **-tion**, **-sion**, or **-ture** to each syllable. Write the word on the line.

1. act   +   ion   =   _____

2. cap   +   ture   =   _____

3. cau   +   tion   =   _____

4. ten   +   sion   =   _____

5. pas   +   sion   =   _____

6. mo   +   tion   =   _____

7. fash   +   ion   =   _____

8. fic   +   tion   =   _____

9. lec   +   ture   =   _____

10. cush   +   ion   =   _____

Directions Choose the word that best completes each sentence. Use the word box for help. Write the new word on the line.

| future |
| invention |
| solutions |
| version |

11. Just one new _____ can make a huge difference to any society.

12. Some inventions provide _____ to problems.

13. Perhaps one new invention will be a new _____ of a computer.

14. What will be the inventions of the _____ ?

© Pearson Education D

Home Activity This page practices words with the common syllables *-ion*, *-tion*, *-sion*, and *-ture*, as in *union*, *potion*, *mission*, and *nature*. Work through the items with your child. Have your child read each word on the page. Then ask your child to divide each word into syllables.

Name_____

Compare and Contrast

- To **compare and contrast** means to tell how two or more things are alike and different.

- Clue words such as *like* and *as* can show similarities. Clue words such as *however* and *instead* can show differences.

Directions Read the passage. Then answer the questions below.

The Olympic Games have been around for a long time. The games first began in Greece in 776 B.C. That is more than 2,700 years ago! They took place every fourth summer in honor of Zeus, king of the gods. Athletes did not compete on teams as they do today. Women could not compete or even watch the games. There were only a few events. Some of them were similar to today's events, such as foot races, wrestling, boxing, and jumping. But others were different, such as chariot races. Winners did not receive medals but wreaths of olive leaves. Like today, athletes were hailed as great heroes.

How are today's Olympic Games different? To begin with, there are winter and summer games. Now the athletes are both men and women. Today, more than 200 different countries compete, not just one. But the biggest difference is the number of sports. In the winter and summer Olympics there are more than 35 different sports. How the Olympics have changed!

1. Name three sports that the modern and ancient games share.

_____

_____

2. Name three major differences between the ancient games and today's games.

_____

_____

_____

Home Activity This page helps your child compare and contrast ancient and modern Olympic Games. Work through the items with your child. Together, read an article about ancient Greece on the Internet or in an encyclopedia. Compare and contrast the way the ancient Greeks lived to life today.

Name_____

Writing

Imagine that you have found an ancient artifact! Think about what this item did for the people who made and used it.

Directions Fill in the chart below to describe your artifact.

My artifact is a _____ .

My Artifact

Looks like...	Used for...	Made from...

On another sheet of paper, write about the artifact you found. Use the ideas from your chart to help you. Make sure to describe what the artifact is and what it was used for. Use interesting describing words.

© Pearson Education D

Home Activity This page helps your child write a description of an ancient artifact. Work through the items with your child. Then help your child find an "artifact" from your home, such as a blender. Discuss what people of the future might think this artifact was used for.

Name_____

Vocabulary

Directions Choose the word from the box that best completes each sentence. Write the word on the line.

Tara was going camping with her Aunt

Sandy. Tara had never camped out in the

1. _____ before. But Aunt Sandy

loved nature and being outdoors. They couldn't

wait for this exciting **2.** _____

to begin. Tara knew the experience would be

3. _____ to her, but she was always willing to try

something new. The night before the camping trip, Aunt Sandy and Tara

checked the weather **4.** _____ . It was going to rain in the

morning! But Aunt Sandy was not worried a bit. "When you plan long

5. _____, you must always be prepared for changes in the

weather," she said, pulling out the rain gear.

> **Check the Words You Know**
> __adventure
> __expeditions
> __forecast
> __unfamiliar
> __wilderness

Directions Circle the word or words with the same or nearly the same meaning as the first word in the group.

6. **unfamiliar**	wild	not known	boring	not fun
7. **forecast**	path	map	prediction	compass
8. **expeditions**	trips	jobs	activities	games
9. **adventure**	task	change	hobby	exciting experience
10. **wilderness**	farm	town	ranch	untamed area

Home Activity This page helps your child learn to read and write vocabulary words. Work through the items with your child. Then have your child tell you about an exciting adventure he or she would like to have. Encourage him or her to use as many vocabulary words as possible.

© Pearson Education D

Name_____

Vowels oo, ew, ue

Directions Write **oo**, **ew**, or **ue** to complete each word. Write the whole word on the line to the left.

_____ 1. Mrs. Serra's neph_____ Joseph flies jets for the navy.

_____ 2. On T_____sday we went to watch an air show.

_____ 3. The airfield is located on Taylor Aven_____ .

_____ 4. The show ended in the aftern_____n.

_____ 5. Joseph flies in one of the n_____est jets.

_____ 6. There was a stat_____ of a pilot near the airfield.

_____ 7. The book has cart_____n drawings of cats.

_____ 8. Amanda bought a poster for her bedr_____m.

_____ 9. Mr. Serra told Jake to stop ch_____ing his gum!

_____ 10. Mom read about the air show in the n_____spaper.

Directions Read the words in each group. Circle the word with the same vowel sound heard in **moon.**

11. untrue	proud	natural
12. famous	withdrew	builder
13. journey	cover	shampoo
14. pilot	overdue	poetry
15. crew	flood	wrong

© Pearson Education D

Home Activity This page helps your child practice words with the vowel sound heard in *soon, blew,* and *true.* Work through the items with your child. Then work together and group the words on this page according to their spellings—words with *oo, ew,* or *ue.*

Sequence

- **Sequence** is the order in which things happen.
- Dates, times, and clue words such as *first, then, next,* and *last* can help you understand the order of events.

Directions Read the passage. Then complete the diagram below.

Have you ever tried scuba diving? Imagine being in a cloud of colorful fish or exploring a sunken ship. What a thrill! But before you hit the deep, you must have training. First, you must make sure you are healthy and have good swimming skills. Then sign up for diving classes. The first diving classes take place in a pool. In class, you'll learn how to take the pressure off of your ears. Then you'll learn underwater hand signals so you can talk to other divers. These signals are very important for keeping you safe underwater. After you pass the pool classes, you'll be taken out for several open water dives. They are usually sea dives. These dives are closely controlled to ensure your safety. Scuba diving classes take a lot of hard work to complete. But when you're done, imagine the adventures you can have!

To Become a Trained Scuba Diver …

- **First**
  ↓
- **Second**
  ↓
- **Third**
  ↓
- **Fourth**
  ↓
- **Fifth**

Home Activity This page helps your child identify the order of events in a passage. Work through the items with your child. Then have your child write instructions explaining how to do something, such as riding a bike or making a sandwich.

Name_____

Writing

Think about what it would take to make an obstacle course in your neighborhood. Think about how you and your friends could work together to build the course.

Directions Answer the following questions about your obstacle course. As you write, think about ideas such as "teamwork" and "working together."

1. What is the name of your obstacle course?

_____

2. List three objects you will use to build the course.

_____

3. List three ways friends will work together to build the course.

_____

_____

_____

4. Describe your obstacle course from start to finish. Make sure to describe the path from start to finish in order.

   a. _____

   b. _____

   c. _____

   d. _____

On another sheet of paper, describe your obstacle course. List the obstacles in order. Make sure to tell how you and your friends can work together to build the course.

Home Activity This page helps your child write sentences about building an obstacle course. Work through the items with your child. Then discuss with your child the way students work together, such as: *Students work together to decorate bulletin boards.*

© Pearson Education D

Name_____

Vocabulary

Directions Choose the word from the box that best matches each definition. Write the word on the line.

_____ **1.** the design of buildings

_____ **2.** changed to fit different conditions

_____ **3.** large area of level or rolling grasslands

_____ **4.** much more than usual

_____ **5.** people who were given land to settle on

_____ **6.** a hole dug in the ground for shelter by an animal

Directions Choose the word from the box that best completes each sentence. Write the word on the line.

7. Most _____ farmed or raised animals on the land the government gave them.

8. Hardly any trees grew on the grassy _____ of the American Midwest.

9. Many desert animals find shelter from the _____ daytime heat of the desert.

10. The prairie dog lives in a _____ it digs underground.

Home Activity This page helps your child learn to read and write vocabulary words. Work through the items with your child. Then invite your child to describe the different kinds of architecture seen in your community.

Name_____

Vowel Sound in *ball*:
a, al, au, aw, augh, ough

Directions Circle each word with **a, al, au, aw, augh**, or **ough** that
has the same vowel sound as **ball**. Write the word on the line.

_____ **1.** Some homes are smaller than others.

_____ **2.** Pick only the ripe strawberries.

_____ **3.** Have you ever thought of racing?

_____ **4.** Did you withdraw money from your account?

_____ **5.** I put the wet laundry in the dryer.

_____ **6.** We shoveled snow from the sidewalk.

_____ **7.** The jeans had to be altered to make them shorter.

_____ **8.** I have a bottle of water in my backpack.

_____ **9.** If you bought a house, how big would it be?

_____ **10.** Who is the author of that book?

Directions Circle the word that has the same vowel sound as **stall.**
Then underline the letters in the word that stand for that vowel sound.

11. braided   daughter   straight

12. walnut   talent   canvas

13. lunch   laugh   launch

14. around   break   thoughtful

Home Activity This page practices words with the vowel combinations *a, al, au, aw, augh*, and *ough*, as in
mall, taunt, crawl, caught, and *ought*. Work through the items with your child. Then ask your child to list words
that rhyme with four of the words circled on this page.

© Pearson Education D

Name_____

Main Idea and Details

- The **main idea** is the most important idea in a passage.
- **Details** are small pieces of information that tell more about the main idea.

Directions Read the following passage. Then answer the questions.

Long ago, native peoples lived in many different kinds of homes. One of the most amazing groups of homes was found in Mesa Verde, Colorado. For about 750 years people lived in homes built right into the cliffs. They are known as "cliff dwellings." Today these cliff dwellings are important because they show the history and culture of early America. Artifacts found in the dwellings show us how early people lived.

The first people there were known as "basket makers" because of the beautiful baskets found there. As time passed, people advanced. They began to make pottery and to hunt with bows and arrows. Many of the homes began as simple adobe shelters. But later more advanced building styles were used. Groups of homes called "pueblos" formed small villages. The Pueblo culture peaked in the years 1100–1300. They built their homes right into the canyon walls. More than 600 of these homes still exist.

1. What is the topic of this passage?

_____

2. What is the main idea of this passage?

_____

_____

3. Write two details that support this main idea.

_____

_____

_____

Home Activity Your child has identified the main idea and supporting details in a passage. Work through the items with your child. Then have your child pretend it is 1,000 years in the future. Help him or her identify items in your home that might show how people of today live.

© Pearson Education D

Name_____

Writing

Think about what it would be like to live in an apartment or in a large single-family house. What are the pros of living in an apartment or a large single-family house? What are the cons?

Directions Fill in the chart telling why each kind of home would be a good or bad place to live. Then answer the questions.

Apartment		Large House	
Pros	**Cons**	**Pros**	**Cons**
1.	2.	3.	4.

5. Do you think it is better to live in an apartment or a big house? Explain your answer.

_____

_____

On another sheet of paper, tell which kind of home you would prefer to live in. Use the information in the chart and the answer to the question to support your choice. Make sure to check for correct spelling and punctuation.

© Pearson Education D

Home Activity This page helps your child write sentences describing which kind of home he or she would like to live in, an apartment or a single-family home. Work through the items with your child. Then invite your child to describe his or her "perfect" home. It can be realistic or fantastical.

Name_____

Vocabulary

Directions Choose the word from the box that best matches each definition. Write the word on the line.

_____ **1.** a special job or task people have been sent to do

_____ **2.** made-up stories that try to explain something in nature

_____ **3.** large holes in the ground shaped like a bowl

_____ **4.** an object that orbits around a planet

_____ **5.** scientists who study objects in outer space

_____ **6.** someone who travels in space

Directions Choose the word from the box that best completes each sentence. Write the word on the line.

Rita has always been interested in the moon, which is a

7. _____ of the Earth. She uses her telescope to look at it

every night. Rita learns from **8.** _____ who spend time

studying outer space. Rita also hopes to become an **9.** _____

in the space program. She wants to be sent on a **10.** _____

to the moon.

Home Activity This page helps your child learn to read and write vocabulary words. Work through the items with your child. Then have your child tell you where in space he or she would like to travel as an astronaut.

© Pearson Education D

Name_____

Suffixes -hood, -ment, -y -en

Directions Add the suffix **-hood**, **-ment**, **-y**, or **-en** to each base word.
Write the new word on the line.

1. state   +   ment   = _____

2. child   +   hood   = _____

3. wood   +   en   = _____

4. rain   +   y   = _____

5. adult   +   hood   = _____

6. chew   +   y   = _____

7. gold   +   en   = _____

8. develop +   ment   = _____

9. father   +   hood   = _____

10. earth   +   en   = _____

Directions Add the suffix **-hood, -ment, -y,** or **-en** to the base word
in ( ) to best complete each sentence. Use the word box for help. Write
the new word on the line.

excitement	
funny	
neighborhood	
silken	

_____ 11. Most people from our
(neighbor) came to the
block party.

_____ 12. I just read a (fun) story about
chickens traveling to Mars.

_____ 13. The crowd cheered with great (excite) when the
team won.

_____ 14. Her (silk) hair was noticed by everyone.

Home Activity This page practices words with the suffixes *-hood, -ment, -y,* and *-en*. Work through the items
with your child. Write some base words and suffixes on separate index cards. Help your child match base
word and suffix cards to make new words, such as *brotherhood, pavement, dusty,* and *leaden*.

© Pearson Education D

Name_____

Draw Conclusions

- You **draw a conclusion** when you form an opinion based on what you already know or on the facts and details in a text.

Directions Read the article. Then answer the questions below.

"That's one small step for man, one giant leap for mankind." On July 20, 1969, Neil Armstrong spoke these words as he stepped onto the moon. He was the first person ever to stand on the lunar surface. People had finally achieved the dream of going to the moon.

People around the world watched their TV sets as Armstrong and his partner Edwin Aldrin Jr. explored the moon. They said the surface was covered with fine powder about two inches deep. Their boots left prints that will last for millions of years! They spent more than two hours walking on the moon. Finally, they planted an American flag in the soil. This showed the world that Americans were the first to walk on the moon. Back on Earth, Americans beamed, smiled, and clapped.

1. What conclusion can you draw from Neil Armstrong's words as he stepped onto the moon?

_____

2. What details in the article support this conclusion?

_____

_____

3. What conclusion can you draw about how Americans felt after seeing their flag on the moon?

_____

4. What details in the passage support this conclusion?

_____

_____

© Pearson Education D

Home Activity This page practices drawing conclusions using details in a short article. Work through the items with your child. Then have your child describe what it might be like to walk on the moon.

Name_____

Writing

Think about different myths or other stories you've heard or read about the moon. Think about writing your own moon myth. Would you write about how it got in the sky? Would you tell a story about its phases? Use your imagination!

Directions Fill in the chart to help write your moon myth.

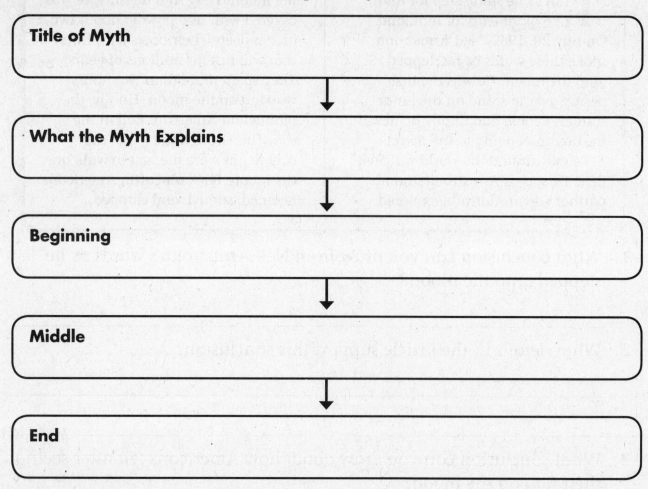

Title of Myth

What the Myth Explains

Beginning

Middle

End

On another sheet of paper, write your myth that explains something about the moon. Your myth can include make-believe characters or just the moon itself. Be creative with your describing words, names, and sentences.

© Pearson Education D

Home Activity This page helps your child write a short myth about the moon. Work through the items with your child. Then invite your child to illustrate his or her myth.

Name_____

Vocabulary

Directions Choose the word from the box that best matches each definition. Write the word on the line.

	Check the Words You Know

Check the Words You Know

__circumstances
__conviction
__devised
__model
__procrastinates
__suggested

_____ **1.** thought up some way of doing something

_____ **2.** puts off doing something until a later time

_____ **3.** conditions that go along with some fact or event

_____ **4.** a small copy of something

_____ **5.** a strong belief

_____ **6.** brought up an idea

Directions Choose the word from the box that best completes each sentence. Write the word on the line.

7. The architect made a _____ of the house he planned to build.

8. He _____ different floor plans for the rooms in the house.

9. A builder _____ changes in the design as the house was being built.

10. The architect said that the _____ were not right for changing the plans.

© Pearson Education D

Home Activity This page helps your child read and write vocabulary words. Work through the items with your child. Then review the words by asking your child to give the meaning of each word without looking.

Short e Spelled *ea*

Directions Choose the word in ( ) that has the **short e** sound as in **head** to finish each sentence. Write the word on the line.

_____ **1.** At first, Tyler (dreaded, needed) running around the track.

_____ **2.** He found running very (unpleasant, unpacked).

_____ **3.** Tyler decided to lead a (healthier, sterner) lifestyle.

_____ **4.** He started running every day regardless of the (weather, beach).

_____ **5.** After a few weeks, he was (really, ready) to enter a race.

_____ **6.** Tyler kept a (straight, steady) pace throughout the race.

_____ **7.** He was (sweating, speaking) when he finished, but he had won first place!

Directions Circle the word that has the same vowel sound as **head**. Then use the word you circled in a sentence.

8. bleach   bread   bleed

_____

9. hearing   healed   heavy

_____

10. feature   freedom   feather

_____

Home Activity This page practices words with the short e sound spelled *ea* as in *head*. Work through the page with your child. Then write the following words: *measure, leather, meadow.* Have your child read the words and use them in a sentence.

© Pearson Education D

Name_____

Sequence

- **Sequence** is the order in which things happen.
- Clue words such as *first, then, next,* and *last* can help you understand the order of events.

Directions Read the following story. Then complete the chart.

Steve wanted to make money in the summer, but he was too young for a real job. One day he got an idea. First, Steve made some flyers. He listed the kinds of jobs he could do, such as taking out trash or caring for pets. Next, Steve walked down his street and left the flyers at every home. Then he waited at home to see what would happen. Before long, Steve started getting calls. Finally, he met with the people who wanted to hire him. Soon Steve had enough work to keep him busy all summer!

The first thing Steve did to get a job
1.

↓

The second thing Steve did to get a job
2.

↓

The third thing Steve did to get a job
3.

↓

The last thing Steve did to get a job
4.

5. What clue words helped you understand the order of events?

Home Activity This page helps your child identify the sequence of events in a short story. Work through the items with your child. Then ask what steps your child could take to find a job or do volunteer work in the community.

Name_____

Writing

Think about a goal a family member or friend has set. For example, maybe a friend wants to learn how to play the piano, join a basketball team, or take dancing lessons. What can be done to meet the goal? What encouragement can be given?

Directions Write the answers to the questions on the lines.

1. Who has a goal? What is the goal?

_____

2. What traits does the person have that will help him or her meet the goal?

_____

_____

3. How can you help the person meet the goal?

_____

_____

4. Pretend you are writing a letter to that person. You want to help the person feel confident about reaching the goal. What will be the first sentence in your letter?

_____

_____

On a separate sheet of paper, write your letter. The letter should offer help and give advice about how to meet the goal. Also tell why you think that person will succeed.

Home Activity This page helps your child write an encouraging letter to a family member or friend. Work through the page with your child. Then have your child read the letter aloud. If possible, let your child share it with the person to whom it is written.

© Pearson Education D

Name_____

Vocabulary

Directions Choose the word from the box that completes each sentence. Write the word on the line to the left.

_____ 1. As a boy Tony was a _____ and quiet person.

_____ 2. He was _____ at himself for being frightened to speak in public.

_____ 3. He set out to change his _____ so he would not be so shy.

_____ 4. He took classes to help him overcome _____ that kept him from speaking in public.

_____ 5. Tony's hard work and _____ finally paid off.

_____ 6. He _____ his goal and today is a speech teacher.

Check the Words You Know
__achieved
__furious
__hurdles
__perseverance
__personality
__timid

Directions Circle the word that has the same or nearly the same meaning as the first word in each group.

7. **furious**	sorry	angry	worried
8. **hurdles**	holes	surprises	difficulties
9. **timid**	shy	poor	tiny
10. **achieved**	learned	accomplished	remembered

© Pearson Education D

Home Activity This page helps your child read and write vocabulary words. Work through the items with your child. Then give clues (such as *this word means angry*), and have your child state the matching word *(furious)*.

Name_____

Vowels *oo* as in *foot* and *u* as in *put*

Directions Choose the word with the vowel sound in **foot** or **put** to complete each sentence. Write the word on the line.

_____ **1.** Did he use a (pulley, probe) or lever to lift the box?

_____ **2.** I (followed, understood) all the steps except the last one.

_____ **3.** Dad is in the kitchen (choosing, cooking) pasta.

_____ **4.** The ship's (lookout, crew) saw no signs of land.

_____ **5.** Many birds make their nests in (bedrooms, bushes).

_____ **6.** Jan saw a (wooden, broken) crate nearby.

_____ **7.** Did you see the weather (bulletin, report) on television?

_____ **8.** Grab a (pillow, cushion) to sit on.

Directions Draw lines through words in the box that do not have the vowel sound you hear in **foot** or **put**. Choose one of the remaining words to match each clue. Write the word on the line.

_____ **9.** a game in which players carry or kick a ball

_____ **10.** a bird with a hard bill

_____ **11.** the opposite of pulling

_____ **12.** a small stream

| baseball |
| brook |
| football |
| pushing |
| river |
| robin |
| tugging |
| woodpecker |

© Pearson Education D

Home Activity This page practices the vowels *oo* and *u* as in *foot* and *put*. Work through the page with your child. Then help your child make a crossword puzzle using words and clues from this page.

Name_____

Draw Conclusions

- **Drawing a conclusion** is forming an opinion based on what you already know or on the facts and details in a text.
- **Facts and details** are the small pieces of information in a story.

Directions Read the following story. Then complete the diagram below by finding facts and details to help you draw a conclusion about Eva's career choice.

Eva loved animals. As a child, she often saved her birthday money to buy animal books and animal posters. When Eva was in high school, she did volunteer work at an animal shelter. The people at the shelter rescued sick and injured animals. Eva spent time watching the vet care for the animals. It made her feel happy when the animals got better. After her work at the shelter, Eva knew what career she wanted. Her parents were not surprised when they found out what she wanted to do.

Facts and Details
1.

Facts and Details
2.

Facts and Details
3.

Facts and Details
4.

Conclusion What do you think Eva wants to be when she grows up?
5.

Home Activity This page helps your child use a graphic organizer to draw a conclusion from a story. Work through the page with your child. Then have your child list his or her interests and talents. Together draw a conclusion about a career he or she might enjoy.

© Pearson Education D

Writing

Think about some of your own goals. Choose one of them and write what you can do to reach it.

Directions Write the answers to the questions on the line.

1. What are some of your goals? If you cannot think of any, the words in the box may give you some ideas.

> **learn a new skill**
> **play an instrument**
> **get better grades**
> **make new friends**
> **read more**
> **play on a ball team**
> **eat healthful foods**

_____

2. What can you do to reach your goal?

_____

_____

3. How can this help you meet your goal?

_____

_____

4. What will make it hard to reach your goal?

_____

_____

5. What can you do if you feel like giving up?

_____

_____

On another sheet of paper, write a paragraph telling about your goal. Explain why you chose that goal. Tell what you plan to do to reach it.

Home Activity This page helps your child write about reaching a personal goal. Work through the page together. Have your child read the completed paragraph aloud. Talk about ways you can help your child reach his or her goals. Make a list and post it.

© Pearson Education D

Name_____

Vocabulary

Directions Choose the word from the box that best matches each definition. Write the word on the line.

_____ 1. the act of coming into a country or region to live there

_____ 2. difficult or embarrassing

_____ 3. to think highly of

_____ 4. something that stands in the way

_____ 5. jobs people do regularly or ways to earn a living

_____ 6. between or among two or more countries

Directions Choose the word from the box that best matches the meaning of the underlined word or words. Write the word on the line.

_____ 7. <u>Act of coming into a country</u> has brought many people to our country.

_____ 8. Many <u>jobs</u>, such as sales, require people to travel during the week.

_____ 9. Your mother will <u>think highly of</u> the extra chores you did.

_____ 10. Falling on the ice was an <u>embarrassing</u> moment for the skater.

Home Activity This page helps your child learn to read and write vocabulary words. Work through the items with your child. Then give meaning clues for vocabulary words and ask your child to identify the words.

Name_____

Long *i*: ind, ild; Long *o*: ost, old

Directions Choose a word from the box that best completes each sentence. Write the word on the line.

almost
older
childhood
golden
behind
postcard
remind
wildly

1. Did you see the _____ Karen mailed to us?

2. The crowd cheered _____ for the team.

3. Who is _____ , you or your brother?

4. Mom doesn't have to _____ Jason to do his chores.

5. The book fell _____ the desk.

6. The actor spent his _____ in the country where his parents had a farm.

7. The queen wore a _____ crown and purple gown.

8. The player _____ caught the ball but dropped it.

Directions Arrange the words in the box by their vowel combinations. Write the words on the lines.

ind

_____

_____

ild

_____

_____

ost

_____

_____

old

_____

_____

© Pearson Education D

Home Activity This page practices words with the vowel combinations *ind*, *ild*, *ost*, and *old*, as in *behind*, *childhood*, *almost*, and *golden*. Work through the items with your child. Then ask your child to make up silly sentences using words from the box.

Draw Conclusions

- **Drawing a conclusion** is forming an opinion based on what you already know or on the facts and details in a text.
- **Facts and details** are the small pieces of information in an article or story.

Directions Read the passage. Then answer the questions below.

From 1820 to 1920, more than 4 million people left Ireland for America. Many people were starving there and couldn't find work. They had heard that America was a good place to start a new life. One of these people was 14-year-old Annie Moore. Annie is famous because she was the first person to pass through Ellis Island. Annie crossed the Atlantic with her two younger brothers. They were meeting their parents in America. As the ship came into New York Harbor, the Statue of Liberty came into view. Annie's heart beat so fast it was pounding in her ears. She could barely catch her breath. A whole new life was ahead of her. As the story goes, Annie Moore passed through Ellis Island on January 1, 1892. It was her fifteenth birthday. Today you can see a statue of Annie Moore on Ellis Island.

1. Draw a conclusion about why Annie's family moved to America.

_____

2. What details support this conclusion?

_____

_____

3. Draw a conclusion about how Annie felt about moving to America.

_____

4. What details support this conclusion?

_____

_____

Home Activity This page shows how to draw conclusions using facts and details in a passage. Work through the items with your child. Then read an article or story with your child and help him or her draw conclusions as you read.

© Pearson Education D

Name_____

Writing

Think about what it would be like to move to a new country. What would you take with you? What items would represent your culture?

Directions Fill in the chart with items you would take to another country.

What I Would Take to Another Country

Food	
Clothing	
Toys/ Games	
Music/ Books	
Other	

Write a paragraph about what you would take with you to another country. Think about the items that best represent your culture. Make sure to use specific details. List several items and tell why you chose them.

Home Activity This page helps your child write about what he or she would take to another country. Work through the items with your child. Then have your child choose several items from around the house that he or she would take to another country. Ask why your child chose each item.

© Pearson Education D

Name_____

Vocabulary

Directions Choose the word from the box that best completes each sentence. Write the word on the line.

_____ **1.** tells that two things are different

_____ **2.** when your mind is made up

_____ **3.** the process of moving forward

_____ **4.** to set to work and stick to it

_____ **5.** able to do something without waste of time, energy, or materials

_____ **6.** doing a good job of moving forward

Directions Write a word from the box that answers each question.

7. Which two words have almost the same meaning?

_____   _____

8. Which word has the most syllables?

_____

9. Which word has the same ending as *ancient* and *sufficient*?

_____

10. Which word rhymes with *reply*?

_____

Home Activity This page helps your child learn to read and write vocabulary words. Work through the items with your child. Then help your child use the vocabulary words to describe a grand gesture.

Name_____

Syllables V/V

Directions Circle the word in each row that has two vowels together where each vowel has a separate sound, as in **piano**.

1. studio   boat   reading
2. reason   creamer   react
3. complain   radio   treatment
4. idea   approach   easy
5. choice   speaker   poet
6. train   museum   heroes
7. tried   cheese   rodeo
8. lion   degree   ready
9. reveal   stereo   applause

Directions Circle words with two vowels together where each vowel has a separate sound. Write the circled words in alphabetical order on the lines.

| green | dread | violin | pioneer | brain | giant |
| video | blue | patio | cloak | cries | triumph |

10. _____
11. _____
12. _____
13. _____
14. _____
15. _____

Home Activity This page practices words that have vowel combinations with two syllables, such as *io* in *audio*. Work through the items with your child. Have your child use each word in a sentence.

© Pearson Education D

Name_____

Main Idea and Supporting Details

- The **main idea** is the most important idea from a paragraph, passage, or article.
- **Details** are small pieces of information that tell more about the main idea.

Directions Read the following passage. Complete the diagram by stating the main ideas and three supporting details.

One grand gesture can cause many good things to happen. Ryan Hreljac (HURL-jak) knows this. When Ryan was six years old, he found out that many people do not have clean water. People get sick from drinking the dirty water. He also learned that a new well can provide clean water. Ryan started saving money to build a well in Africa. He asked other people to give money too. After just one year, Ryan had enough money to build a well near a school in Uganda. Now thousands of people have clean water to drink. But people kept sending Ryan money. So Ryan started a special group called Ryan's Well. Ryan traveled to many places to talk about the need for clean water. As a result, more people gave money to help build wells. Ryan's group has built more than 400 wells in communities around the world!

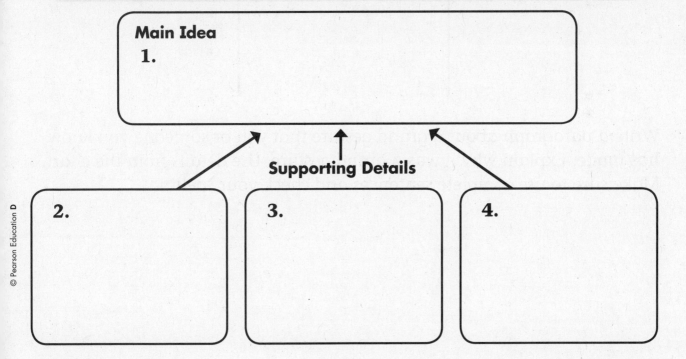

Main Idea
1.

Supporting Details

2.

3.

4.

Home Activity Your child used a graphic organizer to identify the main idea and supporting details of a passage. Work through the items with your child. Then have your child identify the main idea and supporting details for individual paragraphs in a magazine or newspaper article.

© Pearson Education D

Name_____

Writing

Think about a grand gesture you or someone you know has made. Why was it a grand gesture?

Directions Use the chart below to list a few grand gestures you or someone you know did, the sacrifices made, and how people felt.

Helping Others

Grand Gestures	Sacrifices	Feelings

Write a paragraph about a grand gesture that you or someone you know has made. Explain why it was a grand gesture. Use details from the chart. Make sure to use complete sentences and check your spelling.

School + Home **Home Activity** This page helps your child write a paragraph about helping people. Work through the items with your child. Talk with your child about what it is like to make a grand gesture.

© Pearson Education D

Name_____

Vocabulary

Directions Choose the word from the box that matches each clue. Write the word on the line.

_____ **1.** of or related to a time yet to come

_____ **2.** everything that is, including all space and matter

_____ **3.** of or related to science

_____ **4.** device you look through that makes things far away seem larger and nearer

_____ **5.** a group of billions of stars forming a system

_____ **6.** hard to understand

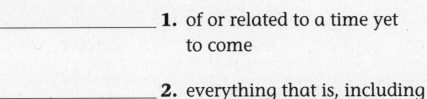

Check the Words You Know

__complex
__futuristic
__galaxy
__scientific
__telescope
__universe

Directions Answer the questions.

7. Which two words in the box have the suffix *-ic* meaning "of or related to"?

_____   _____

8. Which word in the box has the same prefix as *telephone?*

_____

9. What word in the box has the meaning of the underlined words? That is a <u>hard to understand</u> idea.

_____

10. Which is larger, the universe or a galaxy?

_____

Home Activity This page helps your child learn to read and write vocabulary words. Work through the items with your child. Then ask your child to use each word in a sentence.

Related Words

Directions Put a line through the word that is <u>not</u> related to the other words. Use one of the related words to complete the sentence. Write the word on the line.

1. signal   sign   sight   signature

   Please _____ your name here.

2. finish   finger   final   finale

   Do you want to borrow this book after I _____ reading it?

3. vacant   vacation   vaccine   vacate

   We play ball in the _____ lot near school.

4. create   creatures   creative   creaky

   Insect and spiders are living _____ .

5. related   relationship   reliable   relative

   Rob and Jake are _____ to each other.

6. memoir   member   memory   memorize

   I need to _____ this poem for class.

7. describing   descriptive   descended   description

   He wrote a paragraph _____ the race.

8. choose   chose   choir   choice

   You can have your _____ of three colors.

Home Activity This page practices related words, such as *act*, *active*, and *action*. Work through the items with your child. Then ask your child to write a short paragraph using related words from this page.

© Pearson Education D

Name_____

Compare and Contrast

- To **compare and contrast** means to tell how two or more things are alike and different.
- Clue words such as *like* and *as* can show similarities. Clue words such as *however* and *instead* can show differences.

Directions Read the passage. Then answer the questions below.

Mercury and Jupiter are two planets of extremes. Because of these extremes, life cannot exist on either planet. Both planets have been hard to study. Mercury is the closest planet to the sun. It is the smallest planet in our solar system. It is about 1/3 the size of Earth, but it is still visible to the naked eye. Unlike most planets, it does not have any moons. We know that Earth takes 24 hours to rotate once on its axis. Mercury takes about 59 days!

Jupiter, on the other hand, is the largest planet in our solar system. Jupiter is so large that more than 1,000 planets the size of Earth could fit inside it! It is one of the brightest objects in the night sky. Only Venus, Mars, and the moon are more brilliant. Four planets are closer to the sun than Jupiter is. Jupiter has more than 60 known moons. One of the moons is even larger than Mercury! Jupiter rotates much faster than Mercury, about once every 10 hours.

1. How are the sizes of Mercury and Jupiter different?

_____

2. Name things that Mercury and Jupiter have in common.

_____

_____

3. Name things that are different about these planets.

_____

_____

© Pearson Education D

Home Activity Your child compared and contrasted two planets in our solar system. Work through the items with your child. Then have your child compare one of these planets with Earth.

Name_____

Writing

What do you think it would be like to travel in space? Would it be exciting or scary? What kinds of things might you see? Where would you go?

Directions Answer these questions about your trip into space. Use some of the words in the box to help you.

1. In what kind of spacecraft are you traveling?

_____

_____

| galaxy |
| solar system |
| craters |
| atmosphere |
| starlight |
| universe |
| amazing |
| incredible |

2. Who is with you on your trip?

_____

_____

3. Where are you going?

_____

_____

4. Why are you going there?

_____

_____

5. What do you see, hear, and feel?

_____

_____

Write a space log about your trip. Create entries like a journal, with the date and time. Provide lots of interesting details that paint a picture for your readers.

Home Activity This page helps your child write a space log about traveling in space. Work through the items with your child. Then invite your child to read the log aloud so you can share the experience!

© Pearson Education D

Name _____

Reading Log

Date	What is the title?	Who is the author?	What did you think of it?

Name _____

Reading Log

Date	What is the title?	Who is the author?	What did you think of it?

Practice Book

Name _____

Reading Log

Date	What is the title?	Who is the author?	What did you think of it?

© Pearson Education D

Name _____

Reading Log

Date	What is the title?	Who is the author?	What did you think of it?